DATE DUE			

Social
Change
in Complex
Organizations

STUDIES IN SOCIOLOGY

Consulting Editor
DENNIS WRONG
New York University

Social Change in Complex Organizations

JERALD HAGE

MICHAEL AIKEN

Department of Sociology
University of Wisconsin

RANDOM HOUSE
New York

9 8 7 6 5 4

Copyright © 1970 by Random House, Inc.

All rights reserved under International and Pan-American Copyright Conventions. Published in the United States by Random
House, Inc., New York, and simultaneously in Canada by Random House
of Canada Limited, Toronto.

Library of Congress Catalog Card Number: 76-97840

Manufactured in the United States of America

*Respectfully Dedicated
to All Those Who Work for Change*

Preface

The problem of change in organizations has been a major theoretical interest of the senior author ever since his early college days when he tried to introduce changes and did not succeed. This interest has been nurtured with two grants from the federal government that have provided the authors with opportunities to study change and its consequences. The senior author's dissertation was supported by a three-year grant from the National Institutes of Health. The authors' research in the structural factors affecting change was supported by a three-year grant from the Vocational Rehabilitation Administration. We both are deeply appreciative of this support because it has provided us with many opportunities to learn.

A number of women have been helpful in contributing to this effort: Miss Cora Bagley acted as a research assistant on the last project and performed many tasks including the first check on the bibliography; Mrs. Rosemary Ruhde, our secretary, typed several of the earlier versions of the manuscript; Mrs. Lee Abel typed the final versions of the manuscript patiently and accurately, for which we are grateful; finally, Madeleine Hage edited the final manuscript, checked the bibliography, and provided much emotional support during many trying experiences.

A number of ideas have been stimulated by the probing questions of students from whom we have learned much. We hope that this work will in turn stimulate others. It is our wish that this book will be taken as a thank you to all who have aided us.

J. H.
M. A.

Contents

Introduction

PROBLEMS ARISING FROM social change are characteristic of American society. Ours is a society pledged first to
democracy and freedom for its members and second to social
equality and justice for all its citizens. The vehicles for carry-
ing out these ideals on a daily basis are organizations, and it is
not inappropriate that a recent book referred to the United
States as "The Organizational Society." Our economy can be
conceived of as a matrix of several million highly interrelated
organizations—manufacturers, retailers, wholesalers, management consulting firms, stock brokers, regulatory agencies, and
so forth. Our governments—whether the highly complex fed-

eral government or the state and municipal governments—are
organizations that provide services for their constituents. Our
hospitals and medical centers, colleges and universities, are
organizations devoted to providing health, welfare services,
and education to the community.

In a society with such a high degree of social change, problems are continually confronting these organizations. The
problems emanate from such diverse sources as population
growth, technological developments, decisions of international
and domestic governments, and changing values and beliefs
of societal members. Whatever the sources of the problems,
the solutions are likely to require internal change and adjust-
ments in the organizations that carry on the activities necessary for the maintenance of the society and its members. But
organizations vary considerably in their rates of successful
social change. One can appropriately raise the question of why
some organizations are more successful than others in making
the necessary changes that attempt to resolve organizational
problems. This book is an attempt to answer this question.

The answer to the question of why organizations differ in
their rate of change raises a number of other questions that
deserve careful consideration. This study focuses on three
basic questions: What organizational characteristics affect the
rate of organizational change? What environmental factors account for variations in the rate of organizational change? What
is the process of adopting new programs or other changes in
organizations? These three questions are related to the classical
problems in the study of social change: the kinds of change,
the causes of change, and the pattern of change.

Factors That Affect the Rate of Program Change

Seven organizational characteristics that affect an eighth
organizational characteristic—the rate of program change—
will be outlined in Chapter 1. These seven factors are complexity, centralization, formalization, stratification, morale, rate

of production, and efficiency. Welfare agencies, manufacturing plants, research institutes, retail stores, and many other kinds of organizations can be described with these characteristics. These same characteristics also allow us to analyze differences in rates of program change. By considering the impact of complexity, centralization, or formalization on the rate of program change, we can move from description to analysis. The relationships between each of the seven characteristics and program change are discussed in Chapter 2. Each relationship is presented as a simple hypothesis; for example, the higher the complexity, the higher the rate of program change. Rationale and evidence supporting each hypothesis are also presented. In particular, two issues are considered: One, how does a particular organizational characteristic affect the rate at which the initiation of new programs is proposed; two, how does a particular organizational characteristic affect the successful implementation of new programs. The answers to these two questions are, of course, related and provide an understanding of how organizational structure and policy, independently of the desires of the participating members, can either retard or facilitate the adoption of new products and services. The available evidence for each hypothesis involves a variety of organizations, ranging from prisons to hospitals, welfare agencies to business firms.

Dynamic and Static Styles of Organizational Life

Characteristics of organizations do not occur randomly; they are found together in definite patterns. When an organization is high in rate of program change, it is likely to be high in complexity, low in centralization, low in formalization, and so forth. When an organization is low in rate of program change, it is likely to be low in complexity, high in centralization, high in formalization, and so forth. The former type is known as the dynamic style; the latter type as the static style. These organizational characteristics are likely to occur in these two ideal types; that is, we conceive of organizations as social systems that have internal tendencies toward one of these two organizational styles. The simple idea of an organization as a social system provides a number of insights into the dynamics of organizations. By contrasting and comparing the dynamic and static styles, as is done in the first section of Chapter 3, the reader can better understand how organizations achieve their objectives.

Change of the system of an organization, that is, change in the rate of program change, can be conceptualized as the movement between the dynamic and the static style. The change in one organizational characteristic, such as centralization, is likely to result in change in other characteristics. Factors that affect modifications in the program change rate are discussed in Chapter 3 along with several case histories of organizations that changed their style. The major cause of changes in organizational style lies in the environmental elements that an organization must cope with. When there are many rapid changes in its environment, the organization is forced to adapt by altering the rate of program change.

The Process of Adopting New Programs

When an organization's decision makers select a new program or radically alter the rate of program change, they face a series of choices that occur over time. These choices can be viewed as stages. They are evaluation, initiation, implementation, and routinization. As these names imply they refer to the stages of a new program. In the first stage, evaluation, there is the consideration of the need for change. Initiation involves the choice of a solution and the search for resources—both men and money—to pay for the remedy. Implementation involves the actual attempt to start a new activity, and routinization involves the stabilization of the program. Particularly during the initiation and implementation stages there is likely to be a considerable amount of conflict. Not only can change be caused by conflict, but it can create it as well. The leaders of the organization are presented with the dilemma of maximizing change or minimizing conflict. By studying this process in some detail, a better appreciation of the problems of social change in organizations is obtained. The particular choices require the decision makers to select between the alternatives of increasing the extent of the change or increasing the likelihood of acceptance by the participating members. These are hard choices indeed. In the first section of Chapter 4, the stages in the process of adding new programs and the corresponding choices are discussed.

There have been few studies of the actual process of change in organizations. As a consequence, only one extended case history is presented in the second section of Chapter 4. This illustrates the choices and strategies discussed in the previous section. Finally, the chapter ends with a comparison of some other attempts to describe the stages in the process of social change. Although these other efforts differ in the intellectual perspective utilized as well as the unit of analysis, they elaborate our own ideas and clarify them as well. The contrast should make the problems of stages and strategies—an unexplored issue—more comprehensive.

Each of these three closely interlinked problems—change within the system, change of the system, and the process of change—are described in Chapter 5. The complexity of the study of change in organizations becomes even more obvious as additional issues are raised. We have severely limited the scope of variables and the range of topics discussed in this book precisely because of the variety of the issues and problems that would have to be raised to discuss such issues thoroughly. In Chapter 5 some of these limitations are mentioned so that the reader has a sense of the scope of the present study. Such lacunae can provide the direction for future thought and study.

The conclusion of Chapter 5, the last chapter of this study, reverts to the discussion with which we began, namely, the consideration of the evolution of mankind over time as evidenced by the changes in organizational form. On the basis of what we know about the organizational present, as discussed in Chapters 2 and 3, we can look backward into the organizational past and forward into organizational future. Man's main objective remains control over his destiny. This control requires knowledge of where we have been and where we are going as well as knowledge about the consequences of change. This study is concerned with an attempt to codify some of that knowledge.

Finally, progress in the study of innovation has resulted in the publication of a number of studies of organizational change and innovation in the past three years, many of which provide further support for the point of view expressed here, but many of which also address issues not included here. Unfortunately, this book was drafted largely before most of these appeared, which accounts for their seeming inexcusable omission here.

Social
Change
in Complex
Organizations

1 The Anatomy of Organizations

As INDIVIDUALS WE participate in many kinds of social collectives that differ in the number of people involved from the dyadic relationship between two lovers to larger groups, such as families or friendship circles, voluntary associations and organizations, and even to larger units, such as communities and total societies. Not only do human aggregates differ in size but also they differ on many other dimensions, such as the duration of their lives and degrees to which they have recognizable and viable structures. Some human aggregates are short-lived and have little or no structure, such as the rioting mobs that erupted in many urban ghettos during the mid-1960s.

Other human aggregates have longer lives as well as highly formalized and complex structures, for example, the United States Post Office Department. Of course, these are only a few of the many dimensions that students of human aggregates have identified and studied.

Many sociologists call these more enduring and structured human aggregates "groups" and classify them under several general rubrics: primary groups (which include dyadic relationships, families, and peer groups), voluntary associations, organizations, communities, and nation-states. Human aggregates, having shorter longevity and less structure, such as mobs or crowds, are not normally considered to be groups and are often discussed under the heading of collective behavior.[1]

This book is about one type of human aggregate, namely, organizations, although such terms as complex organizations, formal organizations, and large-scale organizations have also been used.[2]

As we advance through life our contacts with organizations steadily increase. Not only do most of us earn our living by working for organizations, but also we are likely to join many voluntary associations. If we achieve some fame or fortune, we may even become a member of the board of directors and help determine policy for an organization. Even if we do not achieve much worldly success, there are a variety of religious organizations to which we can belong and where different criteria of success or failure are likely to be employed. We are clients or customers of hospitals, schools, stores, various government agencies, law firms, and so forth. Even when we die, it is an organization that is likely to handle the entire affair.

This pervasiveness of organizations makes their study an important topic not only for sociology but also for the intelligent layman who wants to understand the world around him. This represents the first reason for the necessity of understanding organizations. Through an appreciation of how organizations operate, it is possible to interpret more correctly the large number of reports that we read in the daily newspapers. A vast part of the news that is reported in such newspapers as *The*

New York Times, Le Monde, or *The Times* involves organizations either directly or indirectly. For example, political and economic events almost always involve organizations; even murders and other kinds of crimes are investigated by an organization. The discussion of the Republican Convention of 1968, the report of labor union activity, or a debate about the United Nations Security Council can be better appreciated when the reader has some knowledge of organizational behavior.

The ubiquitousness of organizations is easily explained; they are the *major* mechanisms for achieving man's goals.[3] This represents a second reason for the necessity of understanding organizations—the more adequate achievement of personal and collective goals, whatever these may be. Whenever there is some specific objective to be accomplished, the realization of that goal requires the development of an organization. The task may be manufacturing hula hoops, registering voters in Alabama, raising money for cancer research, or saving the whooping crane from extinction, but the human solution remains the same—organization. The supporters of a cause must do more than unite. They must organize. The importance of this simple idea was illustrated in an Italian movie *The Organizer.* The tragedy of the film was that the organizer did not know, in fact, how to organize. Because he did not know how, the workers were unable to achieve their aims of a 12-hour workday and higher wages. Instead they suffered much during a long and futile strike.

There is still another purpose in the study of an organization: It is for a clearer appreciation of mankind and his social evolution. Mankind, unlike any other biological organism, has not developed species.[4] Instead, he has chosen the pathway of evolving forms of social organizations. Again, understanding the dynamics of organizational life and, more importantly, their change over time, can provide students with a better appreciation of mankind's evolution as well as a suggestion of how people can exercise some control over their own destinies. Usually discussions of man's control over his own destiny have centered around the control over biological development, rather than control over organizations in society. Yet, the effort of economists, political scientists, psychologists, and sociologists could be one of the most decisive factors in future societies. This is the major purpose of this book: the description and analysis of change in organizations, which may help man to shape his future.

Before we can discuss social change, we need to define an organization and, more importantly, to define an organization sociologically. This is a *sociological* study of change in organizations, not a psychological or social psychological study; but because many readers may not understand the differences between these studies, it is necessary to clarify issues, insights, and emphases of each. In the first section of this chapter organizations are defined, and the difference between a sociological and psychological perspective is discussed.

An organization is more than just a casual sociological definition. Each organization has a number of important characteristics that makes it different from other organizations. The degree of centralization can be used in contrasting and comparing organizations.[5] We can conceive of a characteristic such as centralization varying along some continuum from high to low. For example, the degree of centralization may be high in an army, low in a university, and medium in a manufacturing plant. By knowing how centralized an organization is, we may know something about the operation of the organization both absolutely and relatively. The second section of this chapter defines and illustrates eight organizational characteristics, including program change, which are essential not only for comparisons among organizations but also for the description and analysis of their change.

Definition of an Organization

At the outset of this chapter there was a brief discussion of different categories of human aggregates. One distinction was made between human aggregates that were relatively unstable and unstructured, such as mobs and crowds, and those aggregates that were more enduring and structured. Five different categories of the latter kind of human aggregate were listed: primary groups (including dyads or two-person groups), voluntary associations, organizations, communities, and nation-states.

One way of defining the nature of organizations is to compare and contrast organizations with each of the other types of human aggregates. This method, of course, would require a separate monograph. Instead, we will focus on the differences between primary groups and organizations. Many of the more salient aspects of organizations will become clearer if we first compare organizations with primary groups and later discuss briefly some of the more striking differences between organizations and the other types of human aggregates.

One of the major distinctions between primary groups and organizations is the degree of specification.[6] As the word "organize" suggests, organizations are created and planned to accomplish specific objectives, whether this be the manufacture of products, the care of patients, or the defense of a border.[7] In contrast, primary groups such as families or friendship groups are more likely to emerge spontaneously and are less likely to have specific objectives or goals. The choice of spouse and friends, the ingredients of family and peer groups, are unplanned and have a number of relatively diffuse purposes, that is, emotional support, human contact, or good fellowship. In primary groups the emphasis is often on the enjoyment of the participants. In organizations the emphasis is on getting a job done. It is for this reason that the former are more diffuse than the latter.

It is usually easy to locate an organization because it has a name. General Motors, University of Wisconsin, St. Luke's Hospital, San Quentin Penitentiary, Students for a Democratic Society, United States Army, Sears Roebuck, and the Cubs are only a few examples. Primary groups seldom have a name. As a consequence we usually refer to them by stating who the members are. It is because primary groups often place an emphasis on the non-task related activities that they have no name.

Not only do organizations have specific objectives, but they also have other distinguishing characteristics. Jobs are delineated with a name describing the activities of participating members, such as foreman, boilerman, secretary, auto mechanic, and so forth. The term "job" is never mentioned in the context of primary groups. Who ever heard of job titles for primary group members? Frequently, organizations have a chart specifying the relationships between the jobs in the organizations.[8] There may also be a rules manual which spells out the specific duties, including rights and responsibilities of particular jobs. Organizations, unlike primary groups, usually have charters or constitutions that provide the members with a common frame of reference, namely the specific objectives of the organization.

Some organizations, although not all, carry specification to its logical extreme by adding to their charts, rules manuals, and constitutions, detailed job description books, policy manuals, evaluation systems and a host of other procedures designed to plot every movement and provide every member with a clear prescription of his duties. When a person in one job is replaced, there need be little concern about how he will perform. In contrast, primary groups, especially relatively small ones, do not have this stability because the replacement of one member can make a considerable difference not only in the activities of the group but also in the interpersonal relationships among the participating members.

The extreme in specification is best represented in military organizations such as the United States Navy. On shipboard, for example, there is an activity called general quarters which is designed to protect the ship during attack; its jobs are called battle stations. The duties of the men at battle stations are specified, including words of conversation. Every possible contingency is listed on printed cards along with the appropriate behavior for each participating member. In a word, general quarters is like a gigantic play which is frequently practiced so that all men know their parts.

Although life in organizations is more specific than it is in primary groups, we do not mean to imply that life in primary groups lacks a discernible pattern. Rather, both organizations and primary groups have a recognizable and recurring routine that sociologists can observe, describe, and analyze. The contrast between them comes from the origin of this pattern. In organizations the pattern tends to be planned. The procedures and activities are thought out and articulated to achieve the specific purposes of the organization. In primary groups these patterns emerge over a period of time and the members are less conscious of them. Again, we are not suggesting that every activity in an organization is specified and each behavior in a primary group is left to the vagaries of the situation, but only that primary groups and organizations tend to be in different locations on a continuum of diffuseness and specification.

There are exceptions to every definition. In this case, some primary groups are often organized for the specific objective of the enjoyment of the participating members. The objective may be planned fun or programmed emotional support. In some cases it will be difficult to decide whether a human aggregate is a primary group or an organization. Some primary groups may evolve into organizations; many successful family businesses have experienced this pattern of evolution.[9] Although exceptions exist and are important, the distinction remains useful. The characteristics and activities of primary groups are often diffuse, whereas, the characteristics and activities of organizations tend to have greater specification.

Sociologists have employed many terms in attempting to capture this distinction, at least in part. Among others are gemeinschaft–gesellschaft, primary–secondary, rural–urban, and informal–formal.[10] Each of these continua focuses attention on the consequences of increasing specification in human aggregates. The distinction, regardless of the term used to describe it, is a basic one. This should be remembered because primary groups and organizations are so important in our everyday life. Reality does not always permit such a rigid classification, however. Not all primary groups are more diffuse than all organizations, and some organizations have primary groups within them.[11] Primary groups often emerge spontaneously within organizations precisely because the latter place a greater emphasis on getting the specific objectives accomplished than on the personal satisfactions of their members. The major purpose of this discussion is to underline some fundamental differences between these two types of human aggregates.

Voluntary associations lie on the specificity-diffuseness continuum somewhere between primary groups and organizations. Voluntary associations, including such units as fraternity groups, political parties, and churches, have many attributes similar to organizations, but one fundamental way in which they differ is in the degree of commitment of the members. Voluntary associations often have specific objectives, a formal name, and a charter or constitution, although it is less likely that members, other than officers and committee chairmen, have job titles or that there is a formal organizational chart for the organization. Participation in this kind of human aggregate is likely to be quite limited; that is, although members of an organization may spend most of their working hours with the organization, participation in voluntary associations tends to be more limited in terms of time spent in activities and commitment tends to be less extensive. In short, voluntary associations are less likely to constitute the major life activity for most of its members. Blau and Scott have referred to this type of human aggregate as the mutual-benefit association, but they consider this type of human aggregate to be one type of formal organization.[12] They point out that membership apathy and consequent oligarchical control are two main problems of such associations; these problems grow out of limited participation and commitment. All in all voluntary associations are more similar to organizations than they are to primary groups. For this reason many of the observations about social change in organizations are equally applicable to voluntary associations, although there are clearly exceptions.

Differences between organizations and communities and nation-states are more obvious and therefore require less discussion. Communities are relatively loose social systems that provide a localized population with the major part of its daily sustenance requirements.[13] As such, communities can be conceived of as social aggregates composed of organizations, voluntary associations, and primary groups. Nation-states, or total societies, are human aggregates that are composed of primary groups, voluntary associations, organizations, and communities. The one characteristic of nation-states that differentiates them from these other social units is sovereignty.

Sociological Perspective Versus Psychological Perspective

Any definition of organizations has two major social scientific perspectives that can be used. Organizations can be viewed as an aggregate of individuals, each with his own abilities, interests, behaviors, and motives. This is the essence of the psychological approach. Organizations can also be viewed as a collective of jobs or "social positions," each with its own skills, powers, rules, and rewards.[14] This is the essence of the sociological approach. As a consequence, psychologists and sociologists count differently because there are usually many more individuals than jobs. For example, for the job of foreman, in a manufacturing plant, there may be twenty individuals who work as foremen.[15] In a university, there is one job entitled department chairman, but there may be a hundred individuals who are departmental chairmen.

It goes without saying that in many organizations a number of individuals have two or more jobs. In a hospital one man may be the chief of medicine, director of medical education, and chairman of the committee for medical records. Although it is relatively rare, it is logically possible for the number of jobs to be greater than the number of individuals. Small family businesses are perhaps the best illustrations.

The distinction between individuals and jobs in any concrete organization is relatively easy to determine. Just as individuals have names, for example, Mr. Smith, Mrs. Jones, or Miss Hope, jobs in organizations have titles, for example, chairman of the department, project assistant, administrative secretary, which distinguish them from one another. This distinction between individuals and jobs is not clearly drawn in groups; this is one reason why this form of social life is a favorite focus of attention for the social psychologist who combines both the sociological and psychological approach.

The sociological and psychological perspectives focus on different organizational problems and issues. Sociologists are concerned with such questions as: What are the consequences of particular activities included within a single job? What is the nature of the relationships between jobs? What are the consequences of the particular jobs for the achievement of the organizational goals? or What are the different ways of arranging jobs and what consequences do the jobs have for the survival of the organization? [16] Usually the sociologist relates the characteristics of the job to the functioning of the organization. In contrast, the psychologist is more concerned with such questions as: What are the human limits placed on the work that individuals can do? What kinds of personalities or behaviors are most appropriate for accomplishing certain tasks? How do patterns of perception or thinking influence various organizational processes such as decision making? [17] Usually the psychologist relates the characteristics of the job to the functioning of the individual. [18]

There is a middle road between these two approaches—the socio-psychological perspective, which raises such questions as: Is the right man in the right job? or How do characteristics of the organization affect individual patterns of perception and thinking? [19] Naturally, a total view of the organization requires not only all three viewpoints but others as well, including the economical, political, historical, and so forth. [20]

The focus of this monograph is sociological. The characteristics of organizations discussed in the next section represent sociological variables and problems. This is not to say that this approach is the only one, or even the best one. Both psychological and social psychological approaches raise important questions about organizations. By delimiting our perspective, we shall be able to provide a sharper focus for our point of view. For each of the problems discussed in this monograph, psychological and socio-psychological variables could be utilized. But to do so would make the discussion more complicated. Therefore, only sociological concepts will be considered.

Kinds of Organizational Changes

The purpose of this book, then, is to help students understand social change in complex organizations. We are not concerned with changes in individuals, such as changes in their abilities, interests, behavior, and motives. Instead, we are concerned with the changes in jobs and their arrangements and how these relate to changes in the functioning of the organization. In its broadest sense, social change can be defined as the increase or decrease in any sociological variable.[21] In other words, the topic even within the context of organizations is so broad that it includes almost everything. It is therefore necessary again to limit our focus, at least to begin with, so that our task does not become so diffuse that the reader is left with vague impressions.

Program Change: The Importance of Innovation Program change is defined as the addition of new services or products. A color television product by R.C.A., a molecular biology curriculum at Columbia University, and a mental retardation program in Goodwill Industries are good examples of new programs in organizations. In general, the manufacturers add new products and the service organizations add new services, but in either case there is a new program for the organization, and thus social change.

Why is this kind of change so important? First, because a new program is designed to meet a new need. It represents an attempt, whether successful or unsuccessful, to achieve a goal.

Second, a new program represents a useful way of looking at mankind's evolution over time. One thinks, usually, of the car replacing the horse as a means of transportation or of television ushering in a new era of communication or of the computer altering the ability of man to comprehend large masses of data. These are products produced by organizations, and when first adopted, the products represented a new program, that is, an innovation. Similarly, the service-oriented organizations have adopted many new programs and will continue to do so. Although these new programs are less noticeable, they are equally important for understanding mankind's evolution. The new program may be a rehabilitation program in a prison or a free-lunch program for a school in a slum or a retraining program for the unemployed. This kind of change is important and well worth selecting as our beginning point for the analysis of change in organizations.

Each new program adopted by an organization is not necessarily a success, that is, it does not necessarily solve some organizational problem or meet some need. The new program may create more difficulties than it solves or it may fail to meet adequately the need for which it is designed. In fact, failure probably occurs frequently. The decision makers of an organization must go through trial and error, trying first one new program and then another before they can solve their problem. Business organizations may market many new products before one really is effective in increasing sales. Colleges may try many different courses in attempting to meet student needs. This does not imply that each new program adopted by an organization is necessarily new to the society. A particular new program may be new only to the organization being studied. Borrowing is a very important element in the process of adapting to a changing environment. The therapeutic milieu works in one mental hospital, so other hospitals adopt this program. The navy of one society develops atomic submarines, so the navies of other societies do likewise. In fact, in most cases, programs are borrowed or copied. Although we are concerned with the evolution of organizations, that is, how their structure alters over time, we make no judgment about the relative merits of particular programs. We are concerned with the rate of change in programs and not their success or failure.

The theoretical focus of this book is concerned with the reason why some organizations are quick to institute new programs and even willing to adopt untested ideas; whereas, other organizations are slow to institute program changes and are even unwilling to adopt tested ideas. General Motors and Ford Motor Company had the same environmental conditions during the 1920s but the former organization added new products and the latter organization did not. Even when organizations have the same general objectives and are faced with approximately the same environmental circumstances, we find that there are considerable differences in their rate of program change.

To answer the question of why some organizations successfully implement more new programs than others, it is necessary to locate other sociological variables that can be used to explain and predict variations in the rank of program change. There are at least seven other variables that help explain the varying rates of program change and help define other kinds of organizational change. These seven characteristics are the degree of complexity, centralization, formalization, stratification, production, efficiency, and job satisfaction.

Needless to say, there are a large number of organizational variables that we could discuss.[22] Why choose these seven? There are a large number of sociological studies of organizations that have indicated that these seven variables are highly related to program change, our dependent variable. Although others could be studied, we believe that these are important based on our present state of knowledge about organizations. The nature of each will be discussed more fully in Chapter 2, but let us briefly define each now.

Degree of Complexity: The Importance of Skills   In our society, one of the most commonplace features, so pervasive that many people take it for granted, is the steady accumulation of knowledge.[23] This acquiring of knowledge has led to an ever-increasing number of occupations, each with its own fund of knowledge. Once the family physician was the general practitioner; then he was replaced by the internist, pediatrician, obstetrician, gynecologist, surgeon, and psychiatrist, all specialists.[24] Now these are being supplemented by a bewildering array of medical subspecialists including hematologists, nephrologist, ecologists, endocrinologists, thoracic surgeons, plastic surgeons, radiologists, and so forth. Because most physicians practice in hospitals, the number of medical and paramedical occupations in hospitals has increased greatly. A similar development has occurred in many other organizations, especially those that employ the professions. Professional men place a great emphasis on knowledge.[25]

The number of occupations, especially those requiring knowledge, is a measure of the degree of organizational complexity. If the organization has many occupations, it has high complexity. Hospitals, universities, and chemical companies tend to be high in complexity; whereas, police departments, churches, and many retail stores tend to be low. This feature of organizations is so common that some sociologists refer to all organizations as complex organizations.

The actual enumeration of different occupations in an organization is not always easy. Consider an automobile plant where work has been subdivided into many specific operations, each with its own job title, each with its own worker. The screwing of six door bolts on a car frame all day does not really represent a distinct occupation from the affixing of a pedal on the same automobile, nor do the workers involved consider these tasks to be separate occupations. The precise purpose of the division of work into separate tasks, each performed by different individuals, is the elimination of the necessity for occupations and organizational reliance upon training, skills, and expertise. Therefore, unskilled work does not constitute separate occupations precisely because little knowledge is required or utilized. By our definition, an automobile company or any assembly line manufacturer would likely score low in complexity. Research institutes with many fewer individuals, but many more occupational specialties, would score high and thus have high organizational complexity.

The complexity of an organization is measured not only by the number of occupations but also by the extensiveness of training and intricacy of tasks performed. Some occupations require long periods of training and high levels of skill. Social workers, physicians, lawyers, scientists, are perhaps the best examples of this. The training can be acquired formally in training programs or schools or informally by either apprentice-ship or experience. Organizational sociologists have made much of the distinction between formal and informal modes of social activity. We are suggesting that there are two alternative modes for accomplishing each of the four variables that de-scribe the arrangements of jobs, one a formal mode and one an informal mode.

Variable	Mode		Dimension
	FORMAL	INFORMAL	
Complexity	Training	Experience	Skills
Centralization	Authority	Influence	Power
Formalization	Regulations	Customs	Rules
Stratification	Status	Prestige	Rewards

Thus, a high degree of formalization can be achieved by either regulations or customs. Similarly, a high degree of centraliza-tion can be achieved either through authority or influence. Many occupations actually use a combination of these two methods. Whether the training is formal or informal, the longer the period of required education, the more intricate the occupation; and the more occupations that have long training periods within the organization, the greater the degree of com-plexity in the organization. The degree of complexity can vary even between organizations having the same objectives and jobs. A private welfare agency may hire only graduate social workers who have M.S.W. degrees; whereas, a public welfare agency may employ persons as social workers who do not have any professional training. We would say that the private organization has a higher degree of complexity.

Still another aspect of complexity is the degree to which members of an organization attempt to gain greater knowledge about their respective work activities and the overall activities of their organization. A university that has professors who are active in professional societies and are involved in research has a higher complexity than an organization in which such activities are less. Similarly, an economic organization whose members are involved in various professional, business, and educational activities has a higher complexity than an economic organization whose members are less involved. In each case, activities that reflect greater complexity are those in which members gain greater knowledge and skill. Thus, such activities as these are another aspect of the complexity of an organization.

Because mankind can accumulate knowledge and transmit this knowledge from one generation to the next, he has been able to rely upon social evolution rather than biological evolution. The division of knowledge into separate occupations allows mankind to achieve ever higher levels of expertise and to accomplish ever more complicated objectives. As Durkheim has suggested, such complexity in the division of labor is probably the single best measure of the development of a society.[26] It is also the single best measure of the development of an organization and, thus, of another important kind of change. Parsons has called this change to greater complexity the process of differentiation.[27]

Degree of Centralization: The Importance of Power   The creation of new occupations as a solution to the accumulation of knowledge and as a solution to the achievement of complicated objectives creates other problems. The different occupations or jobs within an organization must be brought together in some system of coordination. Sociologists frequently refer to this as the problem of integration, that is, the problem of tying together all the disparate activities of an organization so that the accomplishment of goals is possible.[28] The creation of a structure arranged on the basis of power is one mechanism of integration. By power we mean the capacity of one social position to set the conditions under which other social positions must perform, that is, the capacity of one social position to determine the actions of other social positions. Power is never a one-way street; every social position has some possibility of setting the conditions of an even more powerful position, albeit modestly. There is a power equation in every set of social actions; the equation must account for the differential power of all participants in the social activity.

The importance of understanding the distribution of power in an organization has been emphasized by several social scientists. In fact, in *The Bureaucratic Phenomenon* Michael Crozier maintains that the key to understanding organizational behavior is the understanding of the phenomenon of power.[29]

Every organization needs to make decisions about the allocation of its funds, the promotion of its personnel, and the initiation of new programs. Responsibilities for these decisions must be allocated to some jobs; this helps ensure coordination of many different occupations. But organizations vary considerably in the way in which they make their decisions. Some place the responsibility for decision making in the duties of a few top jobs, an elite; this is a highly centralized arrangement. Some delegate the responsibility for decision making to lower echelons, allowing many levels of the organization to participate; this is a highly decentralized arrangement. The military, a centralized organization, calls their principle of power distribution the chain of command; the power ultimately culminates in a single job at the top of the organizational hierarchy. The decentralized structure is more like a network of many parts with similar degrees of power.

Although the United States has a creed of democracy, this does not mean that most of the organizations in this country reflect this value in their social arrangements. On the contrary, many organizations are highly centralized. Max Weber, a German sociologist, suggests in his famous model of bureaucracy that centralization is the most rational method.[30] He argues that a more decentralized arrangement reduces control over the individuals who are subordinates, thus reducing the effectiveness of the organization.

It is entirely possible that an organization may have separate arrangements for decision making in each of its major divisions. General Motors uses a combination of centralization and decentralization; the policy and financing are centralized; whereas, operations and product choice are largely decentralized. Such a procedure sometimes disguises the degree of centralization that actually exists in an organization and suggests that some aspects of organization decisions are more important than others. Control of the finances may ultimately lead to control of the seemingly decentralized parts. There can also be entirely different decision-making arrangements for each of the different products or services offered by the organization as well as the different kinds of decisions. But note that when there are different arrangements within the organization, the organization is already partially decentralized, even if the separate sections are highly centralized. An organization in which the accountant makes all financial decisions, the personnel manager makes all personnel decisions, and the plant superintendent all production decisions, is not a monolithic structure. At best it is an oligarchy.

Power can be exercised both formally and informally. Some social scientists call the formal exercise of power, authority and the informal, influence. The holders of certain jobs in an organization have clearly defined rights to give orders to others; this is the authority inherent in their job. For example, the plant superintendent is responsible for making certain limited decisions about the operation of the jobs and machines under his jurisdiction. But all the activities and rights of a given job can never be completely specified for there is always some latitude of action. The occupants of certain jobs in an organization have the opportunity to maneuver within this latitude in such a manner as to persuade others to action. Such opportunity for persuasion reflects influence that can be utilized by a position. Whether power is manifested in authoritative orders or influential suggestions, the decision-making process provides a method for coordinating and combining the many different jobs. The question is where along the decentralized-centralized continuum an organization lies in terms of its internal arrangements. Alterations in the power distribution represent still another important kind of organizational change.

Degree of Formalization: The Importance of Rules Giving orders is only one method for creating a unified organizational effort. An organization could not continue for very long if each operation required a decision from those who have the responsibility to make them. Organizations need daily guidelines for their operations; these guidelines are furnished by rules, the repository of past experience.

The major advantage of rules is that they provide predictability. They specify who is to do what, when, where, and sometimes how. Only junior executives can ride in the elevator, typists must do filing every day, professors may not leave the state without the dean's permission, the executive committee meets every Tuesday morning at 10:00 A.M., reveille for sailors is at 6:00 A.M. except on Sundays: these are just a few illustrations. These rules help specify what each job involves and help create a smoothly operating unit. Weber, who recognized the importance of rules in his model of bureaucracy, likened rules to a machine.[31] Rules make jobs machinelike and coordination efficient; this is their great strength, but it is also a weakness because rules sometimes lead to rigidity and neglect of the social and psychological needs of organizational participants.

In the United States Army, procedures and requirements for military activities are clearly specified and codified in a manual entitled *Army Regulations*. Each unit is required to keep an up-to-date copy in which the multitude of amendments, qualifications, and changes are posted daily. The activities and requirements of military jobs are highly specified and even have military occupation specialty (MOS) numbers. Job description is the term used in business firms to label job specification. One way to determine the degree of specificity of a given job is simply to count the number of rules that define what the incumbent of a job is supposed to do. In fact, the sheer presence or absence of a rules manual is a good indicator of the relative degree of formalization in an organization. If there are a large number of rules or regulations, the organization is highly formalized; if there are only a few, the organization is not highly formalized.

The rules must also be enforced if the job is to be considered formalized. This is not a trivial qualification, because many organizations establish careful descriptions of duties which are promptly and cavalierly ignored. The rules stand as measures of behavior, however, and can be invoked by superiors at their pleasure. Inherent in the duties of many jobs are situations that make the enforcement of job descriptions impossible. Most professionals, for example, teachers, physicians, psychiatrists, social workers, junior executives, salesmen, researchers, artists, and so forth, are in occupations that are structured so that direct supervision is impractical or impossible. Rules for such jobs are less appropriate and can be emphasized only at the risk of introducing some discord into the organization.

Rules are not always written regulations; they sometimes exist in the tradition of the organization as unwritten customs. Many rules are so commonplace that they are forgotten. However, the most important rules usually are codified and written in an organization, especially a highly formalized one. Whether an organization relies on customs or regulations, written or unwritten rules, one way in which organizations differ is in how much emphasis they place on clearly specifying each job.

Increasing formalization can be conceived of as the process

of institutionalization, that is, the process through which rules or customs that regulate social positions and jobs become established. There is some disagreement in the literature on organizations about whether formalization is increasing or decreasing in technologically advanced and industrialized societies. Weber's formulations suggested that bureaucracies would eventually dominate most facets of advanced societies and that formalism, as he called it, would be omnipresent. Some contemporary sociologists, such as Presthus, are of the opinion that bureaucracies, and therefore formalization, are on the increase in industrialized societies.[32] Other sociologists, such as Eisenstadt and Delaney, are of the opinion that formalization is decreasing in industrialized societies.[33] This discrepancy appears to center around the definition of the kinds of rules that are considered. Although the procedures as represented by application forms seem to be steadily increasing, the number of regulations specifying what a person is to do in a job is probably decreasing. There is no logical reason why both of these processes cannot occur simultaneously.

Degree of Stratification: The Importance of Rewards
Power and rules are cohesive forces that help to reduce the disruptions flowing from the presence of different occupational specialties. Another disruptive force that sociologists call a differentiating factor is the distribution of rewards. Some jobs are rewarded more than others; the employees receive higher salary or have more prestige. The stratification system, the way in which rewards are distributed among jobs and occupations, acts as a divisive force in an organization by making job occupants competitive.

In a now famous article, Barnard outlined the importance of stratification within organizations.[34] For Barnard the raison d'être of this social arrangement was its potential for motivating job incumbents to work harder. He reasoned that the desire to reach the top of the organizational ladder would lead to greater work commitment and greater individual effort, and thus ultimately facilitate the organization's achievement of its goals.

Income was not the only reward Barnard envisioned; other rewards such as prestige or esteem could also be employed. For example, in some business organizations the relative importance of vice-presidents can be noted from something so apparently trivial as the thickness of the carpeting in their offices. Often the differential rewards to jobs are intimately connected with the relevance of the job to the accomplishment of the organization's goals. The work of the physician in contributing to the goal of patient care in a hospital is more apparent than is the work of the custodian in the same organization. As a consequence, greater rewards of income as well as prestige accrue to the physician than to the janitor.

The inevitability of some stratification does not mean that all organizations look alike. Some have sharp dividing lines between status levels. The uniforms may be different to say nothing about pay grades. The military has incorporated the principle of stratification as a way of life. For example, the position at meals is carefully calculated on the basis of rank. To a certain extent, every organization has a touch of the military in it. In contrast, some organizations have minimal differences between status levels. In them it becomes difficult to determine the status hierarchy.

The ease of movement from one status level to the next, that is, the rate of mobility, is another measure of stratification within an organization. If it is possible for a man to move from the bottom to the top, then even with sharp status differences the organization has less stratification. Usually mobility is only possible between certain status levels of the organization because of status schisms, to borrow Caplow's term, which act as promotion barriers.[35] If an enlisted man cannot become a general, if the worker cannot become a vice-president, if the nurse cannot become a physician, there is a status schism between occupations in the organization involved.

The formal rank of a job is often called status; the informal rank is called prestige. Status is more likely to be manifested in salaries, whereas, prestige may be indicated by the rug on the office floor, the location of the parking place, or the view from the window. These and other examples of the stratification system in organizations have been amusingly described in a popular work, *The Pyramid Climbers*, by Vance Packard. The important point is that these invidious comparisons between jobs and occupations are important to the participating members. They will work harder to get them and to get ahead.

Amount of Production: The Importance of Achievement
Every organization needs some demonstration of success in order to justify its existence to the outside world and, perhaps more importantly, to its participating members. Salary is not the only reason individuals stay in an organization; most people like to be part of a winning team. Many participating members like to think that their own activities contribute to the accomplishment of organizational objectives. When the organization succeeds in at least partially achieving its objectives, then the members' contributions become more worthwhile.

Within the broad area of organizational achievement, there is a fundamental policy distinction that helps to characterize differences between organizations. Some prefer to increase the volume of production as rapidly as market conditions warrant; whereas, others believe that product quality deserves the highest priority.[36] Mass production industries, such as the automobile, cigarette, and food-processing companies, and craft industries, such as the printing, construction, furniture-making companies, reflect this basic dichotomy in organizational policy.[37] Even within these broad industrial patterns there is considerable variation in specific companies. There are custom-made automobiles and mass-produced furniture. The distinction between an emphasis on quantity or quality applies to other kinds of organizations than manufacturers, although it is easier to see the distinction in this context. Schools, hospitals, prisons, and law firms—any organization that provides a service—has a choice between the relative importance attached to the number of clients served or to the quality of service to the client. Of course the emphasis on quality or quantity is limited by the resources of the organization and by the restrictions of the laws governing it. Some educational institutions are run as if they were factories; others attempt to give quality education to only a modicum of students. Some hospitals are concerned with high quality patient care; others emphasize the number of clients treated. All organizations have some choice between low and high production, between quantity and quality, as a demonstration of achievement.

Amount of Efficiency: The Importance of Resources The degree of efficiency has received a considerable amount of attention, not only in organizational literature, but also in general literature.[38] "How much does it cost?" is a prevalent question in the United States. Efficiency is the measure of how much it costs an organization to provide a service or to make a product. Manufacturers figure the average cost of their products; schools compute their costs per pupil; and prisons report the ratio of guards to prisoners. While the measure of efficiency is usually monetary, it can be expressed in terms of other kinds of costs; for example, prisons sometimes report the use of human resources and armies figure the number of casualties in a battle. In general, money represents a summary measure for many other kinds of resources and allows for comparisons across organizations with different specific purposes.

Although all organizations attempt to conserve their resources because they are scarce, some are much more concerned about their efficiency than others. Some organization decision-makers have an avowed policy of cutting costs. Some organization decision-makers adopt a much more liberal attitude toward this aspect of performance; instead, they worry about other facets of organizational operations. For example, the organization that is concerned about the quality of its product or service or the contentment of its employees is not likely to be so concerned about efficiency.

Amount of Job Satisfaction: The Importance of Morale Although many sociologists look at an organization as a collection of jobs and not individuals, they still must remember that it is human beings who occupy these jobs. The attention paid to collective characteristics does not mean a denial of individuals in organizational life; indeed, the inclusion of the variable of job satisfaction is an attempt to measure the importance of this human element. Organizations must not only conserve their resources; but they must also maintain at least a minimal level of morale and loyalty among employees if they are to survive. Despite the obviousness of this fact, organizations vary considerably in their attitudes toward their employees' morale and well-being. Some have a humane policy; they are concerned about the welfare of their employees both on and off the job. Some have an exploitative policy; they seem to view their workers as part of the machinery. These different organizational orientations, as reflected in company creed and deed have a considerable impact on job satisfaction.

Job satisfaction is a summary measure of many aspects associated with the job, including salary, pace of work, freedom of movement, hours, company regulations, and so forth. Salary is frequently the first working condition considered, but it would be a mistake to assume that it is the only one or even the most important one. In fact, an organization's lack of concern for its employees is best reflected if salary is the main consideration; such an attitude demonstrates an indifferent or exploitative view of the participating members. Some indication of job satisfaction can be found by observing the turnover rates in an organization. If the occupants of a particular job keep quitting, something is probably wrong with the working conditions associated with that job. If this is true for a large number of the jobs in an organization, it probably has a very serious morale problem.

Conclusions

In this chapter we have focused on several words in the title *Social Change in Complex Organizations* and we have attempted to provide some meaning for three of them. For the word "organizations," we have suggested some ways in which it differs from other types of social collectives. The word "social" refers to the arrangement of tasks and the performance of the organization. The word "change" refers to alterations in the arrangements of the various parts of an organization.

To make our discussion of organizational change more concrete and testable, we have selected eight important dimensions of organizational structure and performance. Four dimensions —the degree of complexity, the degree of centralization, the degree of formalization, and the degree of stratification— represent some aspect of the arrangements of tasks which we refer to as structural features of the organization. Three other dimensions—the volume of production, the degree of efficiency, and the state of morale—together with the rate of program change represent some aspects of the functioning or performance of the organization. In discussing these eight dimensions and interrelationships among them, some additional aspects of organizational life will also be introduced.

By the term "organizational change," we mean an alteration in the arrangement of organizational parts, which would be reflected in one of these dimensions. Just as it is important to look at the incidence of change in the number of new programs between a point in time T_1 and a later point in time T_2, so too it is important to look at changes in each of the other seven organizational dimensions during some time interval. The current state of knowledge about organizational behavior is based to a great extent on cross-sectional studies, that is, studies which examine the relationships among various organizational characteristics at some given point in time. While such studies are important and have provided a much better understanding of organizational behavior, at the same time they fail to sensitize the student of organizations to the ongoing process of change in organizations. Organizations seldom stand still; inevitably, change is occuring in the task structure, social relationships, and other aspects of organizational life. A temporal perspective, one in which the focus of attention is not only on the interrelationships of parts of organizations, but more importantly on changes in these interrelationships, is ultimately necessary for a more complete understanding of organizational behavior. It is such changes in the arrangements of organizations—especially in the eight dimensions outlined above—that is of primary concern in this book.

2 Program Change: The Problem of Change Within the System

IT IS STRANGE that American sociologists have not studied program change more than they have. The United States is a society that is continually experiencing a very rapid rate of development. Manufacturers continually produce new models. Governmental agencies allocate large amounts of money for research and development. Fads and fashions are a persistent phenomenon of the society. And the competition between organizations is a part of the American ethos. In view of these factors, and others, most organizations in the United States, regardless of their goals, exist in a changing environment and must make continuing appraisals of the implications of these changes for the organization. Despite this, the problems of organizational change have not been studied in depth by American students of organizational behavior. The most extensive American research on the problem was done by a group of educators under the direction of Paul Mort, but in our judgment the best single empirical work was done in Scotland by Burns and Stalker.[1]

There are few studies that explicitly analyze organizational change; however, many studies implicitly discuss this phenomenon. We have reviewed a large number of theoretical and empirical works in order to isolate those factors that relate to this problem.[2] We have also engaged in an extensive research study of our own in order to test some of the specific hypotheses discussed in this chapter.[3]

Each hypothesis in this chapter—there are seven altogether —relates program change to one of the other seven organizational characteristics. For example, we hypothesize that the higher the complexity of an organization, the higher the rate of program change. This and the other hypotheses are not randomly formulated, but instead are based on a theoretical understanding of organizations.[4] Our justification for the plausibility of each hypothesis is discussed in a section of this chapter. We shall offer for each hypothesis a variety of reasons that reflect our understanding of how organizations operate.

In our theoretical discussion of each hypothesis, two problems in the study of program change will be considered. The first is whether a specific variable, for example, complexity, is related to the *initiation* of new programs. The second is whether a specific variable facilitates the *implementation* of new programs. There is an obvious connection between these two problems. Decision makers in organizations learn from past experience and base many of their decisions on that experience. If organizational leaders decide to initiate a new program and if they experience considerable difficulty in the process of implementing it, they may abandon it and perhaps avoid initiating future programmatic changes. In other words, we do not always make the argument that all organizations successfully implement programs that are initiated. Some specific organizational arrangements make the process of implementation smoother than others; and, therefore, organizations with these arrangements will become more favorably disposed to future changes. Thus, it is worthwhile distinguishing between those characteristics that facilitate the *initiation* of new programs and those that facilitate the *implementation* of them. Despite their close interrelationship, the solving of each of these two problems could require different organizational circumstances.

A word of caution is owed the reader at this point. Although the structure of our argument will be to show how a number of organizational characteristics are associated with the initiation and implementation of new programs, it is not our view that the dynamics of organizational life always flow in only one direction. We conceive of an organization as a social system; that is, in a state of moving equilibrium. Perhaps the reader can best visualize this by making the analogy to a basket of nervous ping-pong balls, full of unreleased energy, suspended in a given configuration. Should something happen to upset the position of any one of these, all will ultimately be affected, and a new equilibrium will eventually occur. For convenience of argument, we shall systematically look at these ping-pong balls (organizational characteristics) one at a time to show how they affect the ball marked "change"; but we must point out that each of our arguments could be reversed. We could just as well start with the "change" ball, assume that its relation to some other ball is altered, and then trace out the influence on the other ping-pong balls in the basket. In other words, we do not infer one directional causality, but rather a high degree of interdependence among organizational parts.[5]

Complexity and Program Change

Rationale The complexity of an organization refers to the level of knowledge and expertise in an organization. There are two complementary aspects of complexity: the number of occupational specialties in an organization and the degree of professionalism of each. In other words these two dimensions of complexity reflect both the extensity and intensity of knowledge in the organization. The longer the period of training for the occupation, whether formal or informal training, and the greater the number of occupations that are professionalized, the more complex the organization. Thus:

■ *The Greater the Complexity, the Greater the Rate of Program Change*

"Professionalism" is an increasingly familiar term in an advanced industrial society such as the United States. One writer has recently posed the question of whether everyone is becoming a professional in our society.[6] Although many usages of the term refer primarily to the spread of tenure arrangements, licensing and certification, or increasing specialization, we, like Wilensky, conceive of professionalism in terms of autonomous expertise and adherence to a service ideal in which there is a devotion to the clients' interests more than to personal or commercial profit. Expertise requires both training and experience. The service ideal impels men to seek new knowledge continually in order to serve the clients' interests more adequately. Professionalism implies an insatiable appetite for knowledge, and this acquisition of knowledge leads to the recognition of how little we really know about the world we live in and even our own fields of specialization. It inspires us to greater learning. In a sense, then, knowledge is by definition self-generating.[7] An organization that has many varieties of professionally trained persons is likely, therefore, to bear witness continually to these internal pressures toward change.

The more emphasis that a job in an organization places on the acquisition of knowledge, the more concerned the employees will be with keeping abreast of developments in the field. Physicians not only subscribe to a large number of professional journals, but they also periodically attend refresher courses designed to inform them about recent medical advances. Even the military has a war college where war tactics are studied by ambitious generals. One consequence of this continued education, this accent on knowledge and reeducation, is the recognition of the need for change. Advances in knowledge mean new programs and techniques. Thus, the physician requests a new radioisotope scanner for blood research and testing, the college professor suggests a program in the sociology of developing nations, and the business manager advocates the establishment of a public relations department. A high degree of complexity in an organization brings about great pressures for the initiation of new programs and procedures in an organization. We would argue that under such circumstances of great organizational complexity, these newly initiated programs and procedures are also likely to be introduced successfully into the organization.

The addition of even one new occupation can result in the proliferation of ancillary occupations. As an illustration of this phenomenon, an endocrinologist was added to a staff of a community hospital. Not only was a new laboratory tests and procedures apparatus subsequently added, including the purchase of radioisotope equipment, but lab technicians skilled in biochemistry as well as persons qualified to operate the newly acquired equipment were hired. Education programs had to be instituted to inform the physicians and paramedical personnel of the availability of these new tests and procedures. It is unlikely that the addition of a public relations expert to a hospital staff would have had the same organizational consequences for the hospital. In other words, occupations vary in terms of the degree of their impact on organizational change. In general, the greater the amount of knowledge associated with the occupation, as indicated by the length of formal and informal training, the greater the likelihood of ancillary occupations also being added. Consider the impact of the addition of a cyclotron to a research institute or a high-speed computer to a business firm. In each case greater complexity is likely to result and, of course, the greater the number of highly trained occupations in an organization, the greater the probability of new programs being added.

The sheer number of occupations itself represents a dynamism leading to more change. The greater the number of different occupations, the more diverse the perspectives and values of the members within the organization. Each occupation will compete for its fair share of organizational power and rewards. From this occupational conflict can come the impetus for change. Each occupation will attempt to demonstrate the necessity for its programs, and this encourages the process of their seeking new ways to improve organizational performances. In addition, the sheer number of occupations creates problems of organizational coordination. This results in positive efforts towards the development of programs in order to solve these problems of coordination. Thus the emphasis on communication techniques in complex business organizations, on information storage in medical libraries, and on the development of multidiscipline research teams in research institutes are examples of attempts to coordinate the diversity of occupations that are found in complex organizations. Some new jobs that are not normally considered to be separate occupations have emerged as a consequence of the problems created by complexity, especially when disparate branches of knowledge are involved.

Evidence Not unexpectedly, most of the available evidence to support our hypothesis is found in research studies dealing with organizations of great complexity, namely, schools and hospitals. The most extensive research on organizational change has been done by a group of researchers under the direction of Paul Mort at Teachers College, Columbia University. This group developed a scale of "school adaptiveness" that consisted of 176 new educational practices covering a variety of areas from administration to curriculum.[8] School systems were examined and their characteristics related to varying rates of adoptions of change. In one study involving forty-three school systems, adoption of new teaching techniques was found to be highly correlated with the amount of professional training and experience of teachers.[9] What is especially interesting about this particular study is that change in educational practices was higher in those schools with the highest rates of teachers' reading and travel. This research suggests that not only the level of training, but also continued education practices, such as reading and travel, are important in providing a stimulus for organizational change.

A case study of a community hospital found that the introduction of a new occupational specialty was most readily accepted in those medical departments that had a higher proportion of specialists than in those departments staffed primarily by general practitioners and in those departments with a history of change, as measured by the number of successful program innovations during the previous five-year period.[10] Of course, these two factors themselves were highly related, that is, a history of many successful program changes was most likely to have occurred in the departments staffed by many specialists. We studied sixteen welfare agencies in a large metropolitan community—ten private and six public—that provided services involving physical rehabilitation, mental rehabilitation, or psychiatry.[11] In this study, organizational complexity was measured in the following ways: the number of occupational specialties in each organization, the length of professional training required by each specialty, and the degree of involvement in professional societies and activities of each specialty. The correlation coefficient between the number of occupational specialties in the organization and the number of new programs added during the previous five-year period, that is, the rate of program change, was .45. Professional activity, which was measured by the number of professional associations the respondent belonged to, the proportion of meetings attended, and the number of papers given, also had a correlation coefficient of .38 with the number of program changes. Similarly, the amount of professional training was positively related to the rate of change in organizations, although the size of the correlation was somewhat less. In other words, regardless of the particular measure of complexity, there was a positive relationship with the number of program changes.

We have suggested that one of the major reasons for the relationship between complexity and organizational change is that conflict among different occupational specialties gives rise to the development of new programs. In a study of Scottish electronics firms, Burns and Stalker found that there was considerable conflict over the allocation of organizational resources as well as the development of many new products in those firms that placed greater emphasis on person specialization.[12] Other supporting evidence is provided in a study of research groups by Pelz.[13] He found greater creativity, thus greater change, in those research groups with a high frequency of interaction between researchers with dissimilar academic training. But perhaps the best demonstration of this is a case study of the occupation of purchasing.[14] When practitioners of this occupational specialty attempted to increase their autonomy as a separate occupational activity, the job incumbents became involved in conflicts with other departments. These conflicts occurred not only because of the attempts of members of the purchasing departments to participate in organizational decision making, but also because of attempts to increase the number and scope of activities associated with the job of purchasing in a business firm, that is, the number of new programs and activities.

As the reader will note, most of our examples refer to the successful implementation of new programs. Obviously, there is a tendency for researchers to be less sensitive, and less eager, to relate unsuccessful attempts of program change. We have little proof for our assertion of greater initiation of new programs under conditions of high organizational complexity, but ample documentation for successful implementation of new programs under such circumstances.

One exception, a case study of a community hospital, followed the addition of the same program into four different departments.[15] A teaching ward service was successfully implemented in the department of medicine but not in surgery. What differentiates these two different departments is the degree of complexity. The medical department not only had a much higher proportion of specialists than did the surgical department (in which a high proportion of the physicians were general practitioners), but also the medical department had a much greater variety of specialists as well. Although some programs were successfully implemented in both departments, in each case the process was shorter in the medical department than in the surgical department. At the same time, the degree of medical specialization does not explain all the differences between the departments. Pediatrics, which had a higher degree of specialization than the department of medicine, had more difficulty in implementing new programs than did medicine.

Centralization and Program Change

Rationale Centralization refers to the way in which power is distributed in any organization. By power we mean the capacity of one actor to move another (or other) actors to action. The smaller the proportion of jobs and occupations that participate in decision making and the fewer the decision-making areas in which they are involved, the more centralized the organization. Thus:

■ *The Higher the Centralization, the Lower the Rate of Program Change*

This hypothesis refers primarily to the successful initiation of new programs; we shall discuss the issue of implementation later. The concentration of power in the hands of a few persons in the organization tends to lead to the preservation of the status quo because one aspect of power is the ability to veto ideas for change or otherwise block attempts to introduce change into an organization. Such a viewpoint assumes that those who have power conduct themselves in such a way as to enhance, or at least maintain, their present power. This idea is usually called the "iron law of oligarchy," which maintains that organizations are essentially undemocratic in their practices.[16] Changes in the activities of an organization may lead to alterations in the power equation in the organization, and thus it is arguable that organizations in which a few individuals monopolize power may experiment less with changes in programs or techniques.

An organization with low centralization has a decision-making arrangement that allows for the representation of different occupational perspectives, thus permitting the interplay between different interests and ideas. The strain toward change contributed by complexity of the organization is enhanced when the diverse elements implied by that complexity are found in a decentralized organization. Participation of diverse occupations in decision making often takes place in committees which can be a forum for both the proposal and the creation of new programs out of the clash of opposing viewpoints. Although decentralization encourages the process of occupational conflict inherent in a complex organization, it also facilitates the initiation of new programs and techniques, whether the source of the idea is internal or external to the organization. A more generalized statement of this principle is that democratic decision making implies not only limited, but omnipresent, conflict among participants. This frequently leads to high rates of social change. Conflict within a previously defined set of boundaries is to be valued rather than feared, especially if the social changes resulting from the conflict lead ultimately to beneficial changes in the organization.

An organization with a high degree of centralization is one that has a decision-making arrangement in which top administrators may veto proposals for change. This is not to say that centralized organizations are always static, but in general they are more likely to be slower in initiating change. In a centralized organization there are few channels of communication from organizational members on lower levels to the elite of the organization. In addition, there is sometimes an air of secrecy in a centralized organization. When new programs are proposed by lower specialists in the organization, the decision to adopt these proposed programs is likely to be long and arduous because of insufficient opportunities to dramatize the need to organization decision makers. Even if new products or services are approved and initiated, the period of implementation may be similarly delayed because of communication difficulties. As a consequence the decision makers may be uninformed of problems that inevitably occur during the implementation of new programs. Necessary communications are likely to be retarded until the chances for failure are unalterably increased. This may discourage any future attempts with new programs.

Evidence   The scales of adaption, or in our terms "program change," developed by Paul Mort and his associates, were also used in a study of innovation in sixteen centralized and sixteen decentralized schools in New York State by Cillié.[17] The sixteen centralized schools were all part of the New York City school system; the sixteen decentralized schools were autonomous school districts in villages and communities just outside New York City. The schools were matched on geographical location, financial expenditures, socioeconomic status, racial distribution, and a number of other factors such as class size, teacher preparation, and teacher salaries. Cillié found that the decentralized schools had adopted more new programs than had the centralized schools. For example, he found that the decentralized school systems had continuous revisions of courses of study, more experimentation with new methods, and more recent instructional materials. What is especially interesting about his findings is that the adoption of new programs and techniques by these decentralized schools increased their capacity for change and flexibility, resulted in greater individual attention to pupils, allowed a greater scope of instructional services, and permitted the teachers to participate to a greater extent in decision making. In other words the specific kinds of new programs or techniques were anything but random. They were likely to include procedures that increased complexity and further decreased centralization. In contrast, when the centralized schools adopted new programs, they more often chose those practices that increased efficiency, not those that would result in greater decentralization and complexity.

Support for this hypothesis is also suggested in a cross-national study by Ben-David of organizations conducting medical research.[18] Ben-David noted that the organization of medical research activities in Great Britain and France was more centralized than in the United States and Germany. Medical research in the latter countries was decentralized among many private and state universities. He found that the rate of development of new medical techniques and discoveries was greater in the United States and Germany than in Great Britain and France. Social change in the development of new medical techniques and programs was not altogether absent in these countries with more centralized medical research; rather, it simply occurred at a lower rate than in countries with decentralized medical research. Although this example was not a study of organizations per se, it well illustrates the validity of our hypothesis, using slightly different units of measurement.

The U.S.S.R. has been conducting some experiments in the decentralization of its economy during the last decade.[19] Until 1957 the Gosplan was prepared in the central office of the ministry. This plan specified detailed objectives for every sector of the economy, including each organization; amounts of raw materials, wages, process, and a number of other parameters were included in the plan. In 1957 Nikita Khrushchev, then head of the government, complained about the lack of diversification in products, particularly in the chemical sector. His diagnosis of the problem was that there was too much centralization; therefore, he ordered the establishment of one hundred regional economic councils that were largely autonomous. The consequence of this action was an increase in the number of products and a proliferation of new programs and techniques. This trend towards decentralization was given added impetus in the latter part of 1964 when the Soviet Union accepted the proposals of economist Evsel Liberman and detached approximately four hundred light-industry plants from rigid central planning.

Single case studies of organizations, always subject to considerable qualification with respect to their representativeness, are nevertheless sometimes more revealing than more sophisticated comparative research because they permit a greater focus on some of the details involved in a particular hypothesis. Lipset's study of the coming to power of the Cooperative Commonwealth Federation (C.C.F.) party in Saskatchewan is a case in point.[20] Although the party had been elected on a program involving a number of specific proposals for new programs and although the elected officials were committed to these, the centralized bureaucracy was largely effective in blocking many changes. In part, this was the result of the higher-ranking members of the civil service maintaining that certain proposals were impractical or had been tried and found ineffective. In part, this occurred because of a difference in values especially of the higher echelons in the civil service. Regardless, proposals, even when instituted, were frequently ineffectively implemented.

In our study of sixteen welfare agencies, the staff members were asked how often they participated in organizational decisions regarding the hiring of personnel, the promotions of personnel, the adoption of new organizational policies, and the adoption of new programs or services.[21] The score for each organization was based on the average of participation in these four areas of decision making. Measured in this way, decentralization had a correlation of .49 with the rate of change in new programs. Agency-wide decisions are not the only kind that are made. Other decisions are those concerning the performance of a specific job. Agency-wide decisions are basically those concerned with the control of resources; job decisions are basically concerned with the control of work. The latter was measured by a scale called the hierarchy of authority. The correlation between this kind of centralization and the rate of program change during the previous five-year period was −.09. In other words, the centralization of power of decision making over organizational resources was more important than the degree of control over individually assigned jobs.

Formalization and Program Change

Rationale   Formalization refers to the degree of codification of jobs in an organization. The greater the number of rules specifying what is to be done, whether formally written or informally understood, and the more strictly they are enforced, the greater the formalization of the organization. Thus:

■ *The Greater the Formalization, the Lower the Rate of Program Change*

Rules set limits not only on what men do but also on what men think. Rules are not only the repository of man's past experience, but they may become the bulwark against future proposals. A highly formalized job provides little latitude to the occupants of the job for considering alternative procedures or practices. As a consequence, little initiative is likely to be exercised. In fact, to take initiative may get the employee into trouble for not following the prescribed routine. Rules thus encourage conformity and discourage new ideas or suggestions. In the extreme, ritualism, an organizational pathology in which a job occupant compulsively follows the rules, is likely to become the prevailing mode of behavior for job occupants.[22]

Rules not only discourage new suggestions or new patterns of behavior because of the possibility of getting into trouble, but they also discourage the search for better ways of performing the same tasks. There is the implicit assumption by the creators of organizational rules that any rule represents the best way of performing a certain task or the preferred method for achieving a certain objective. This assumption is often readily accepted by job occupants. In contrast to a well-defined job, an ambiguously defined job actually encourages the occupants to look for new methods and techniques perhaps for no other reason than to provide some predictability in their own work and to escape the anxiety which may result from too much discretion. In one sense the paucity of rules, that is, low formalization, may spur organizational change because of the search for some guidelines of behavior by those who dislike their ill-defined situation.[23]

Rules may retard the implementation of new programs as well. The more rules there are in an organization, the more likely a new product or service is likely to run foul of them by making conflicting demands on the individuals involved. Whether an individual opts for obeying a new rule or for fulfilling the needs of a new program, the organization is likely to experience some difficulties. If the rule is obeyed, the program may be retarded or possibly even sabotaged. If the rule is not obeyed, there may be a temporary interruption of service in the organization. Experiences such as these—conflict over rules, breakdowns in organizational functioning, and other such consequences that flow from the implementing of change in a formalized structure—discourage an organization from attempting future changes.

Evidence   There have been surprisingly few studies of the relationship between rules and program change, despite the commonplace observation that bureaucracies, the citadel of rules, are resistant to change. In our study of sixteen welfare organizations, we attempted to measure the degree of formalization in two different ways.[24] The first measure is a scale determining the degree of job codification and the second measure is a scale designed to gauge the degree of rule observation. The job-codification scale attempts to determine the sheer number of regulations that specify who is to do what, when, and where. The rule-observation scale attempts to determine the sheer diligence in enforcing who is doing what, when, and where. The latter is an important qualification because many organizations may not enforce all their own regulations. Job codification was found to have a negative correlation of −.47 with the rate of successful implementations of new programs in the previous five years. Rule observation, however, had no association with the rate of change in organizations.

Stratification and Program Change

Rationale Stratification of an organization refers to the differential distribution of rewards to the jobs in an organization. The types of rewards that are differentially allocated to organizational positions are usually money and prestige. Prestige may take a variety of forms such as title, office size, location of office, type of desk, and so forth.[25] The greater the difference between the top and the bottom, whether the differences are in terms of salaries or prestige, and the harder it is to move from bottom to top, the greater the degree of stratification in the organization. Thus:

■ *The Greater the Stratification, the Lower the Rate of Program Change*

Those who have greater wealth and prestige in an organization are less likely to favor new programs and techniques if the change diminishes the status differences among jobs and occupations.

This hypothesis is an old one and has been stated by many sociologists in other contexts. It was central to Karl Marx's theory that the bourgeoisie, the owners of the means of production, would attempt to preserve the status quo in any capitalist society. In his famous discussion of the functions and pathologies of status systems, Chester Barnard indicated that a high degree of stratification is likely to be associated with little change.[26] His discussion probably represents the first exposition of this hypothesis in the organizational literature.

The main theme running through Marx and Barnard is the idea that any change is likely to result in a reallocation of rewards. The men at the top of the stratification hierarchy, that is, the ones with the most rewards, are likely to be the ones most affected by innovation. Therefore, there are understandable reasons of self-interest for their being opposed to change. But resistance to change is likely to be in evidence only when there are considerable differences in rewards within the organization because the less the stratification, the less effect new programs can have on the relative distribution of rewards. When there are only minor differences in salaries and prestige, the organizational members who occupy the top jobs have little to lose by supporting new programs.

Although it can be expected that the men at the top of a highly stratified organization would be likely to veto proposals for change, this is not the only way in which a highly stratified system can limit program change. Barnard argued that the main purpose of a stratification system was to provide lower-rewarded members with a clear line of promotion with ever-increasing rewards. This supposedly would motivate them to work harder. But at the same time this principle discourages suggestions for change because implicitly, if not explicitly, criticisms of present arrangements are criticisms of those who instituted them. Therefore, a highly stratified system discourages proposals for change from the members desirous of promotion.

High stratification has crucial effects on the channels and networks of communication between jobs in an organization. It discourages upward communication, especially information about inadequate performances and is also associated with reduced horizontal communication between departments within the organization. The competition between members is one reason for this lessened horizontal communication. Such a system sometimes leads each man to look out for his own best interests with the consequence of secrecy about inadequate performances.

It would be erroneous to imply that the lessened vertical communication, as a consequence of stratification, represents only a reluctance to avoid displeasing superiors. Generally, communication between unequals, whether in terms of status or power, is restricted. People feel most comfortable when speaking to their equals; they will seek them out, especially for emotional support.[27] The more sharply distinctions are drawn between jobs, the less likely it is that interpersonal communications will develop. In *The Organization Man,* William Whyte has elevated this idea to the level of a principle, namely, the admonition to avoid friendships with peers because you may become their boss the following year. This attitude also discourages the mutual interchange of ideas that may generate new programs.

Evidence   There are few organizational studies that cover a long time period. Ben-David's examination of medical research is probably the record holder; it covers 125 years.[28] Ben-David indicates that the organization of medical research was highly stratified in France and Great Britain. One man tended to dominate a particular specialty, and there was little change in this situation over time. As a result, there were few innovations in medical practices. Such a high degree of stratification did not exist in Germany and the United States. The latter added new medical specialties, developed new techniques, and adopted a more crucial change in the organization of medical research, namely research laboratories. France and Great Britain did not. A particularly interesting point made by Ben-David is that it was not the lack of information about innovations that reduced the rate of change in medical practices in France and Great Britain; instead, it was the blockage to change created by the characteristics of their medical organizations. High stratification discouraged the introduction of new programs and inhibited the development of the medical profession. Bright men were encouraged to go to other disciplines that offered clearer and more promising paths to fame and fortune.

A number of small-group experiments have shown that when a group is attempting to determine the best idea in a process of innovation, status differences seriously hamper the successful outcome of the process.[29] Because the novel situation, which is a consequence of changes in technical or market conditions, corresponds to the group situation in which the task is to find the best answer, these studies lend credence to the hypothesized negative association between the degree of stratification and the rate of organizational changes. Several studies of organizations indicate that there is a general reluctance by lower ranking job occupants to criticize the ideas of their more powerful or prestigious supervisors.[30] This attitude has obvious adverse consequences on rates of program change.

Some circumstantial evidence is provided in a study by Berkowitz and Bennis.[31] They found that high stratification reduced interaction in science-oriented organizations. And if interaction is reduced, then the opportunities for conflicting ideas to be heard is blocked. Shephard and Brown in another study of research organization found that stratification affected rates of interaction adversely both within and outside the organization.[32]

In a case study of change Ronken and Lawrence studied a plant making electronic equipment.[33] They found that status differences retarded the actual implementation of a new product, a new vacuum tube. What is provocative about their findings is that the organization recognized it had communication difficulties and eliminated several intervening authority levels between the plant superintendent and the foreman. The latter was instructed to report all problems directly to the superintendent. Still, the foreman was reluctant to talk about his difficulties because of the differences in status; the former did not recognize the problem, and the consequence was a slowdown in the implementation of the new product. Status differences not only discourage the initiation of new programs, but they also retard their implementation.

Production and Program Change

Rationale   Production refers to the relative emphasis on the quantity or quality of the organization's products or services. A high volume of production implies an emphasis on quantity; a low volume of production often implies an emphasis on quality. Thus:

■ *The Higher the Volume of Production, the Lower the Rate of Program Change*

When organizational policy emphasizes the speed of production and volume rather than quality and control, decisions are likely to be made that will avoid the interruptions that are a perennial by-product of innovation. In organizational contexts in which there is emphasis on high volume of production, organizational decision makers are less likely to perceive any need for changing the existing arrangements.

To paraphrase an old cliché, nothing fails like success. The organization with a high volume of production is likely to be resistant to the development of new products or services. The rationale used by organizational elite is that if production is high, everything is functioning adequately. Under these circumstances, it is less likely that anyone will raise a question of whether improvement is necessary.

Evaluation of organizational programs is most typical when an organization is concerned about quality of its outputs. A quality standard is a most elusive performance measure and provides a continuing impetus for change. For example, each new discovery in patient care is likely to be immediately investigated and often adopted by a hospital that is concerned with its quality. A manufacturing company that watches the quality of its products is likely to maintain a research department specifically for the purposes of improving its manufacturing techniques and processes; this is usually called research and development.

When a new program is implemented in an organization, there is a period of trial and error before it is successfully incorporated into the organizational repertoire. During this period of implementation, there is likely to be an adverse effect on existing production; and the higher the volume, the greater the drop. Entire assembly lines, a technique characteristic of high production manufacturers, have to be shut down in order to change one operational method. This fact results in strong organizational resistance to continuous change. The sheer number of difficulties that any change in routine would unleash discourages the initiation of change. In contrast, the disruptive effects of change in techniques are much less in an organization in which there is little emphasis on high volume of production.

Evidence   There is little evidence to support this hypothesis because researchers have not seen it appropriate to relate these variables in their studies. However, some inferences can be drawn from the 1964 *Statistical Abstract* of the research budgets in different types of industries. The cigarette, chemical, food, and automobile industries—those with a high volume of production—allocate a relatively small proportion of their budgets to research and development. In contrast, aircraft and electronics—those industries with a low volume of production—allocate a relatively large proportion of their budgets to research and development.

Efficiency and Program Change

Rationale   Efficiency refers to the relative emphasis on the cost reduction of the product or service. The cost may be counted in men, money, space, time, or some other resource. A high degree of efficiency implies great organizational efforts to conserve resources; a low degree of efficiency implies little organizational effort to conserve resources. Efficiency has been referred to as one aspect of "organizational effectiveness" by some researchers.[34] Thus:

■ *The Greater the Emphasis on Efficiency, the Lower the Rate of Program Change*

New programs usually not only represent additional costs of operation, but if they are truly innovations, they also represent unpredictable costs. The actual implementation of change always reduces the efficiency of an organization because of the disruptions in routine which change implies. Therefore, organizations that are concerned with maximizing efficiency are more likely to opt for a continuation of the status quo. Of course, changes in the organization's environment may force the organization to alter certain of its procedures or products.

Some innovations are designed to actually increase efficiency. Unfortunately, the fact that they are usually only spending more of one resource in order to save another is sometimes overlooked. A factory may automate in order to cut labor costs, but in the process it may spend exorbitant sums of money on machines and space. Even if there is a net gain in efficiency, there is considerable difference between organizations that adopt new programs or techniques for the purposes of improving quality as opposed to improving efficiency.[35] Most new programs are concerned with the former and not the latter. Therefore, organizations that are concerned about efficiency will likely have a slower rate of program change.

It is unlikely that an organization that is concerned about its costs will try radical departures from traditional methods because the operational costs incurred are unpredictable. In such an organization there sometimes occurs a "wait and see" policy towards new products or services in order to determine the appropriateness of the change as well as its costs. The cautious organization will have a slower rate of program change because all innovations are not successful, nor do they represent progress. Organizations with a high rate of program change may even have a number of programmatic failures. This means lower efficiency, regardless of which resources we may examine in measuring reduced efficiency.

Evidence   Buley found that those schools with high rates of program change had higher per pupil expenditures.[36] Cillié, using the same empirical scale of adoption or change, found that those schools with high rates of program change more often adopted programs that provide for more individual attention to students.[37] Zald, in a study of correctional institutions, discovered that those institutions with higher staff-inmate ratios developed a greater number of programs for their clients.[38] In general, any organization—for example, a prison, hospital, school—that is concerned with the quality of its service is likely to introduce more programs, but at a higher cost.

A case study of the addition of the assembly line for a new electrical tube provides a number of illustrations of how expensive innovation is during the period of implementation.[39] The costs were high at first because the specification of jobs was impossible; time was spent trying to find the most effective operations and procedures. The demands on the organization made by the requirements of the assembly line had an impact on the efficiency of operation in other areas mainly because the innovation required extra time and attention from a variety of jobs that entailed other responsibilities.

Job Satisfaction and Program Change

Rationale   Job satisfaction refers to the degree of morale among the job occupants in an organization. It covers a variety of aspects in the working conditions, including pay, hours, fellow workers, superiors, and so forth.[40] High job satisfaction across all jobs in the organization implies an organization with high morale; low job satisfaction implies an organization with low morale. Thus:

■ The Higher the Job Satisfaction, the Greater the Rate of Program Change

People who are satisfied with their jobs are more committed to the organization; consequently, they are more receptive to new ideas for improving existing products or services. These same people are also likely to be willing to try innovations suggested by others.

It could be argued that the contented job occupant will be complacent; instead, job satisfaction really suggests a pride in work which is reflected in the continued effort to improve the quality of work. This effort may lead to the development of changes or alterations, those trifles that add up to perfection. The necessity for having high morale during a period when new techniques or programs are being implemented is frequently overlooked. Change creates strains because it affects organizational habits and customs. In addition, stress and strain are common at this period in an organization's life. Machines may break down, programs may alter, and tempers are likely to flare. Only if the organization has high morale can it successfully implement the new activity and weather the ensuing organizational stress.

Evidence   Probably one of the most significant experiments in the organizational literature documents the finding that workers more readily accept change when the job satisfaction is high.[41] In this particular study, the changes were relatively minor ones; yet there was still considerable resistance to the changes because of low job satisfaction. When working conditions were altered by allowing the workers to participate in decisions about the proposed changes, job satisfaction increased and innovations were accepted readily. (The way in which working conditions facilitate program change will receive greater attention in Chapter 4.) As a consequence, not only was implementation easier, but also the workers proposed a number of changes themselves, facilitating organizational change even more.

Gouldner's study of a gypsum plant is in part a case study of how low job satisfaction can seriously hamper attempts to change an organization.[42] Mr. Peale, the new plant manager, was effectively blocked in anything he attempted to do. The study is an excellent illustration of how sheer force, the power of promotion and demotion, or pay increases and decreases, does not guarantee that change can be successfully implemented.

Peter Blau's famous case study of two state welfare agencies suggests that favorable working conditions and, more importantly, higher job satisfaction make the implementation of change much easier. The study also indicates that satisfied workers also contribute to change by initiating suggestions.[43]

In our study of welfare agencies, we measured the level of job satisfaction and the level of satisfaction with fellow workers and supervisors.[44] The former measure had a correlation of .38 with the rate of program change during the past five years, but the latter measure had a correlation −.17 with program change. In other words the organizations with higher rates of change had higher work morale but less satisfaction with social relationships than organizations with lower rates of change. These correlations suggest a plausible explanation for several contradictory viewpoints concerning morale and organizational change in the literature. Coch and French have suggested a positive relationship between morale and change; however, a series of studies done by Mann, Hoffman, and others at the University of Michigan have noted that change creates strain for the job occupants who experience it.[45] Our findings suggest that job satisfaction is a necessary precondition for the introduction of changes, but once a change has been introduced, it can have disruptive and negative effects on social relationships among the members of an organization. It is also plausible to argue that the organizational conditions that facilitate the introduction of change, namely the diversity of occupations and decentralization, may reduce satisfaction with social relationships because of the conflicts that they engender.

Case Study of an Organization with Low Program Change

In this chapter we have discussed how each of the seven organizational characteristics—complexity, centralization, formalization, stratification, production volume, efficiency, and job satisfaction—is related to the rate of change in products or services. Most of the illustrative evidence cited above has been taken from diverse studies that considered only one or two of these organizational characteristics or properties as they were related to program change. A study that considers all the properties as they are found in an unchanging or static organization would undoubtedly be more convincing. One highly static organization has been described by Michel Crozier in *The Bureaucratic Phenomenon.*[46]

Crozier describes the Parisian branch of a large governmental agency. The main activity of the agency is the clerical processing of voluminous financial transactions. To say that the organization was highly static is certainly no understatement. Crozier reports that the technology of the agency was relatively simple and had remained virtually unchanged for the past thirty-five years. He describes the tendency towards rigidity in the organization and the resistance to social change.

The organization was almost completely a "line organization," that is, there was no staff at the branch level, meaning there were practically no professionally trained personnel. In fact, there were only three types of nonsupervisory personnel. The organization had a very low degree of complexity as we have defined it. In addition, the organization was highly centralized, with a quasi-military chain of command. The director and assistant director of the agency had a great degree of power, although even greater power was attached to the parent body of the branch. Not only did the organization have low complexity and high centralization, but understandably there was a great reliance on rules and routines. Discretionary decisions by supervisors were usually avoided; instead, rules were relied on whenever possible to solve organizational problems. The organization was also highly stratified, and great differences in rewards were allocated to the occupants of different strata in the organization, leading to crystallization of these strata. Communication between strata was relatively absent or ineffectual. The presence of a staff often serves to facilitate communication between upper and lower levels in an organization; but because this clerical agency had no staff, this avenue of communication was also absent.

A general feeling of malaise characterized the vast majority of workers in the agency. Almost 90 percent were dissatisfied with their jobs in the agency, and such low morale led to a relatively high rate of turnover in personnel—15 percent per year. The average seniority in the organization was only three and one-half years. Of course, this is partially a consequence of most employees being young females. Because of the pressure from above, there was a heavy emphasis on productivity— quantity at the expense of quality. The heavy work load, of course, was a contributor to the malaise in the agency. There was a great emphasis placed on thrift and cost reduction, and this attempt to reduce overhead expenses, to conserve resources as much as possible, meant the organization placed a high premium on efficiency.

It is not difficult to understand why there was so little change in such an organization. The emphasis on rules and routine, the lack of adequate channels of communication, the isolation of strata, a quasi-military chain of command, and the low degree of knowledge resulted in high job dissatisfaction, high turnover of personnel, an emphasis on productivity and efficiency, and the virtual absence of any impetus for change. Crozier reasons, and we would agree, that it would take some cataclysmic event to alter the organization. He also argues that the ethos of this organizational climate reflects a larger cultural ethos, suggesting that organizational forms in France are probably quite different from the American or Russian models. We are less inclined to agree with this, because we feel that these hypotheses are likely to be valid in all societies. French bureaucracies may perhaps be more formalized, but this could be predicted from knowing other attributes of such organizations. What Crozier has described is an excellent example of the inner dynamics of organizational life working out a logical and equilibrated arrangement of its parts.

Case Study of an Organization with High Program Change

The profile of the highly static organization described by Crozier can be compared with a study of highly dynamic organization that comes from our own research on program change in social welfare and health organizations. The Rehabilitation Workshop was started in 1919 to provide treatment and rehabilitation for physically and mentally handicapped persons. At its inception this private organization offered primarily physical and occupational therapy for children and adults. Over the years services have been greatly expanded, and today the agency offers a wide assortment of services for people having physical, mental, and social disabilities.

In order to provide such diverse services, the organization has gathered together a highly diversified set of employees, from speech therapists to neurologists to social workers. In fact, in 1966 there were thirty-seven different types of occupational specializations in the organization. Many of these occupational specialties require advanced degrees, M.A.s, M.D.s, and Ph.D.s. Not only does the organization have an unusually high number of highly trained and disparate occupational perspectives, but the persons filling these roles are quite active in their various professional societies in terms of holding offices and giving papers at professional meetings. In fact, among the sixteen organizations in our study, the Rehabilitation Workshop ranked second, fourth, and second highest respectively in terms of number of occupational specialties, the degree of professional training of incumbents, and in the degree of professional activity. In short, the organization has a high degree of complexity as we have defined it in this book.

The Rehabilitation Workshop is relatively decentralized; most organizational members participate frequently in organizational decision making. The actual mechanism of this participation is a highly active committee structure. There are six permanent committees in the organization, each of which meets once a week. These meetings bring together members from all parts of the organization to solve an array of problems. In addition, ad hoc committees are frequently formed to consider special problems.

There is little formalization of the Rehabilitation Workshop. Among the organizations in our study only two others placed less emphasis on the close supervision of their employees. Similarly, the organization was below the median in terms of the rigid codification of work activities. This is not difficult to understand; highly trained professionals must be given maximum discretion and autonomy in completing their assigned tasks. During one of our interviews a work adjustment counselor at the Rehabilitation Workshop volunteered that she enjoys working in the organization because of the freedom allotted the staff. There is a system of rewards in the organization, but it does not emphasize differences among levels as much as some organizations. In other words, the stratification of the Rehabilitation Workshop is lower than in many organizations.

In terms of the morale of the organization, the Rehabilitation Workshop is much higher than most other organizations in our study. Over seventy-five percent of organizational members reported they were "very satisfied" with the various aspects of their jobs when we interviewed them. Specifically, this meant that they felt that their jobs were better than similar jobs in the community, felt that they were accepted as professional experts, and were satisfied with their present jobs in terms of their career expectations. In addition, organizational members reported very high satisfaction with their fellow workers and with their supervisors. Only in two other organizations was there greater satisfaction on this measure. In short, morale was exceedingly high in this organization.

The quality of client services was much more important both to the head of the organization and to the organizational members than the number of clients. In the words of a middle-level staff member of the Rehabilitation Workshop: "We are being put under pressure to expand, but we've held back to maintain quality." Not only is there a value commitment to quality of services rather than the number of clients served, but also the actual quality of client care is exceedingly high. This organization enjoys an unusually high reputation among other organizations in the community for the effectiveness of its programs; in fact, Rehabilitation Workshop was given the highest ranking by the executive directors of the sixteen organizations in our study.

We do not want to suggest that there are no problems in the organization. Of course there are some staff members who are dissatisfied with their jobs and the organization. In most cases, however, this is a result of staff members being unhappy with the salary and fringe benefits of the Rehabilitation Workshop in comparison to business and industry. Such problems are endemic to most private health and social welfare organizations in our society, however.

In comparison to the other health and social welfare organizations in our study, the Rehabilitation Workshop is characterized by a high degree of complexity and a low degree of centralization, formalization, and stratification. In addition, there is little emphasis on productivity or efficiency. But what about the degree of program change in the organization, our measure of a dynamic organization? During the period from 1959 to 1964, the organization introduced six new programs, a rate of program change that was exceeded only by two other organizations. Similarly, during the next three years, 1964 to 1967, the organization introduced five new programs. Once again only two organizations had higher rates of program change. Among new programs added were a new training program in building maintenance, a recreation club for stroke patients, and an evaluation program for deaf children. There were more programs planned for the future. This organization planned to continue to add new training programs and to expand the range of handicapped children evaluated.

Many of the new programs of the organization were joint programs with other agencies. In fact, the Rehabilitation Workshop had been involved in over thirty joint programs with other organizations in the past ten years. Many of these joint programs involved the training of professionals—for example, social workers, occupational therapists, rehabilitation counselors, internists—with the major universities in the area. As a consequence the Workshop was not only highly complex, but was also continuously exposed to new ideas via these relationships with other organizations. Some of these joint programs involved ongoing research projects designed to find new solutions to the problems of rehabilitation.

Thus, the organization was not only highly dynamic but also highly oriented to quality. While other organizations may have had more new programs, the Rehabilitation Workshop implemented programs that increased the quality of its services, each program filling a logical gap in the organization's services. Change was not an end, but a means towards creating an even more effective organization.

Conclusions

In this chapter, our approach has been to focus on one single problem: the rate of change in new programs and techniques or the problem of change within the system. Specific hypotheses have been suggested that relate seven organizational characteristics to program change. This simple procedure has at least two advantages. First, the procedure makes it easier for the reader to evaluate critically the line of reasoning that has been used. Second, it facilitates the reader's weighing of the evidence cited. In this way, the reader can judge both the face validity as well as the empirical validity of our seven hypotheses. But this is only part of the story of change in organizations. In the next chapter we shall discuss not change *within* the organizational system, but change *of* the organizational system itself.

3 Styles of Organizational Change: The Problems of Change of the System

MOST ORGANIZATIONS FOUND in highly industrialized societies eventually need to incorporate at least a few new programs, techniques, or activities in order to survive in a constantly changing environment. But there is considerable difference between the business firm, prison, advertising agency, or hospital that is the first to innovate and one that is the last to imitate. In Chapter 1 we called the former type a "dynamic" organization and the latter type a "static" organization.

We can describe these two "ideal types" of organizations in terms of the eight dimensions discussed in the previous chapter. These characteristics do not occur randomly, but rather they seem to cohere in certain configurations of organizational characteristics. In other words, there is a certain internal tendency toward either the static or dynamic configuration. If the reader will visualize the extremes of these eight organizational characteristics as sixteen nervous ping-pong balls suspended in a basket, that is, a ping-pong ball marked high centralization and another marked low centralization, and so forth, then we are suggesting that eight of these ping-pong balls will cluster together in the "static" side of the basket and the others will cluster on the "dynamic" side. For example, both the high specialization ball and the low centralization ball are likely to occur together as parts of the highly dynamic style; whereas, low specialization and high centralization will cluster together as parts of the highly static style of organizational life. The characteristics of these styles are discussed in the first section of this chapter.

Organizational decision makers can consciously choose to make the organization either dynamic or static, and organizational policies can also be shaped by a variety of circumstances external to the organization. By examining some of these, predictions can be made as to when a particular kind of organization is likely to tend toward either the dynamic or static style. A specification of some of these important circumstances in the environment also allows us some basis for predicting when an organization may alter. For example, if because of changing marketing conditions sales for a product fall, we may anticipate movement from a static to a dynamic style. Some important characteristics in the environment are discussed in the second section of this chapter.

An understanding of how an organization evolves into either the dynamic or static style implies an understanding of how the organization operates as a social system. In the third section, several case histories are presented to give the reader a feeling for the daily reality of these types of organizations and how they change.

Dynamic and Static Organizational Systems

We have suggested that organizations are social systems. For our purposes a *social system* is defined as a set of variables that are interrelated so that a change in one variable results in or is associated with a change in another variable. Again the variables can be visualized as ping-pong balls. A change in one will eventually affect the others. We call this a social system because each of the variables represents an abstract dimension of interactions among people. The degree of centralization, for example, represents an arrangement of decision making; it is a variable abstracted from organizational life.

Perhaps the concept of a social system can be best understood with a simple illustration from another field, meteorology. Our weather can be, and is, described by a set of physical variables—such as temperature, air pressure, humidity, cloud coverage—so arranged that they form a system, a weather system. There are two general types of weather called the cold air mass and the warm air mass. If the temperature falls, the air pressure rises, the humidity decreases, and the cloud coverage lessens; then we know that a cold air mass has arrived. The characteristics of temperature, air pressure, humidity, and cloud coverage are said to be interrelated because a change in one is associated with a change in another. Actually the weather system of variables is much more complex than this. The kinds of clouds, the direction of wind, the wind force, and a number of other characteristics are additional variables in the system. The important point is that a change in one variable will change the others because they are interrelated. And so it is with a social system.[1]

Just as there are two ideal types of air masses, we can visualize two ideal types of organizational systems that can be characterized by the eight variables. In the previous chapter we related program change to each of the other organizational characteristics by examining seven specific hypotheses. In this section the interrelationships between the eight characteristics of the dynamic style and the static style are discussed. Since the latter model is the reverse image of the former one, a better grasp of each is obtained by discussing them separately. Neither style is necessarily superior to the other; each has its strengths and its weaknesses. After examining the interrelationships among the eight variables, other characteristics of the two styles are briefly discussed. These come from the development of two models of organizational life—the organic form and the mechanical form—based on research in electrical firms in Scotland.[2] By combining the characteristics of these two models of organizations with our characteristics of the dynamic and static styles, a much richer understanding of organizational life is obtained.

Dynamic Style   The organization with a high degree of program change has a number of logically consistent and interrelated parts. The more complex the organization is—that is, the more that an organization relies upon the use of a variety of occupational specialties that require a long training period —the more likely the organization is to be low in centralization. As knowledge increases, it becomes increasingly difficult to invest power in a few elite positions or jobs. Decisions must increasingly be made after consulting different specialists; in the process, the specialists informally influence decision making, even if they should not be invested with formal authority. Can the chief administrator of a hospital really make an intelligent decision about the purchase of new surgical equipment without consulting the chief surgeon? The more advanced the training of the members of an occupation in the organization, the more difficult it becomes for those in authority positions to supervise or otherwise control the work of specialists.

Advances in knowledge not only create pressures toward the dispersion of power, but they also create pressures toward the elimination of many rules governing the behavior of job occupants. It becomes increasingly difficult to break complex skills into simple operations that can be rigidly specified in a job-description manual. As Thompson has noted, there is a movement from task specialization to person specialization, with reliance increasingly being placed upon the expertise and skill of the job occupants.[3] The professional occupations are perhaps the clearest example of this trend in the United States. Jobs performed by such professionals as teachers, physicians, lawyers, managers, scientists, or social workers are not easily reducible to separate and simple operations requiring little training. As a consequence, organizations that utilize occupations requiring long periods of either formal or informal training depend upon the quality of that training instead of rules as the means of ensuring predictable job performance. Concomitantly, the occupants of these occupations attempt to ensure as much latitude for individual initiative as they possibly can, that is, they attempt to achieve autonomy in order to make their own decisions and thus be less constrained by organizational regulations and customs.[4]

The specialist, the individual with training, usually establishes informal channels of communication in the organization which cut across hierarchical lines of authority. This communication is necessary because he needs access to different departments in order to discharge his duties as a trouble shooter. The consequence is not only a loss of control by those in elite positions, but also the diminishing of status and prestige differences among the various occupations.[5] As knowledge expands and organizations become more complex, it becomes increasingly difficult to argue that one job or occupation is more important than another. The sense of teamwork that is a part of a complex organization helps to diminish further the status and prestige differences among various jobs and occupations.

The structural arrangements of a dynamic organization are high complexity, low centralization, low formalization, and low stratification. Associated with these structural arrangements are usually certain general organizational policies. Members of occupations that require long periods of training are likely to advocate an emphasis on the quality of the product or service provided rather than on the organizational efficiency. Specialists often make demands for the improvement in the quality of work, demands that are reflected in new programs, new techniques, and rising costs. They are also likely to make demands for the improvement of their own working conditions, demands that are reflected in higher job satisfaction and additional increased costs. Moreover, highly trained specialists are much more likely to be happy with their working conditions than those who have less training because they have more autonomy and fewer rules as well as less status and prestige differences. In other words, dynamic organizations are likely to be decentralized, to lack formalization, and to place little emphasis on stratification. These dimensions of organizational structure and organizational policy complement one another, reinforce one another, and therefore tend to cluster together in the same organizations.[6]

Few organizations would fit the model of the dynamic organization exactly. Rather we see in organizations having certain of these properties a strain toward the development of the others, or, to use our analogy, we see a tendency for attraction among the ping-pong balls reflecting these properties. Of course, factors external to the organization may set in motion contradictory tendencies. If this occurs, the organization presents a mixed picture. Contradictory tendencies often occur in organizations, indicating that the organization is in a state of flux. In the long run, however, there will be a tendency toward the ideal type of the static organization if certain of these properties exist in an organization. We would speculate that certain organizational characteristics may be stronger than others in the tendency toward the dynamic style, but that will be discussed later.

Static Style   The logic of the development of a static or relatively unchanging organization is quite different. The less complex an organization, that is, the more that an organization relies upon the use of task specialization instead of person specialization, the more likely it is to be high in centralization. Instead of relying upon the expertise and the skill of job occupants, there is the attempt in the static organization to break jobs into a variety of simple operations that can be performed by unskilled labor. Job descriptions, rules manuals, evaluation systems, and a host of documents and records are printed so that everyone knows what they must do. This emphasis on formalization means that decision making can be located in a few elite power positions whose occupants supervise the performances of the other job occupants in the organization, thus maintaining social control. The rules provide the standards by which both job and organizational performances can be compared.[7] As a consequence, there are likely to be great differences in status and prestige among various levels in the organization, depending upon how much responsibility for decision making, rules formulation, and supervision of subordinates the particular position has. The elite are likely to overestimate the significance of their contributions to the achievement of organizational objectives and underestimate the significance of the contributions of other job occupants in the organization. The occupants of powerful positions are likely to distribute rewards such as pay or office space disproportionally, maintaining a strict hierarchy of authority as well as status and prestige.[8]

Thus the characteristics of a highly static organization are low complexity, high centralization, high formalization, and high stratification. The general policies of such organizations are likely to emphasize the quantity of the product or service provided as well as the efficiency in the production. An emphasis on production requires little evaluation, but an emphasis on the quality of production is much more costly. A high volume of production lends itself to a reduction in per unit cost—high efficiency. As a consequence, if power is located in a few positions, there is likely to be little consideration of the working conditions of the other members. The inevitable consequence of this is likely to be low organizational morale. Lack of autonomy, many rules, and status differences can create dissatisfaction even when organizational policy may be favorable to high organizational morale. Again we see that organizational structure and organizational policy tend to match each other;

the policy justifies the structure and the structure conforms to a certain type of policy.

Organic Model Versus Mechanical Model   The differences between these two styles of organizational life have not gone unnoticed. On the basis of extensive research experience, Burns and Stalker arrived at somewhat similar models of organizational life.[9] They labeled their two models the organic form and the mechanical form. The organic model is characterized by "the adjustment and continual redefinition of individual task" (low formalization) and a network structure of control, authority and communication" (low centralization); it is similar to our dynamic style. The mechanical model is characterized by "the precise definition of rights and obligations and technical methods attached to each functional role" (high formalization) and a "hierarchical structure of control, authority and communication" (high centralization); it is similar to our static style. The organic model relies upon the special knowledge and experience of individuals, person specialization; whereas, the mechanical model relies upon the differentiation of tasks into specific operations, task specialization; that is, the former model is high in complexity and the latter model is low in complexity.

We have suggested that a dynamic organization is low in stratification, but Burns and Stalker suggest that the organic model is still stratified according to expertise, not according to authority. On this point there is some divergence between their work and ours. They state, however, that leadership in particular situations is assumed by the most informed and capable—the "best authority." This indicates a shifting system of prestige—status depending upon the nature of the skills needed—which implies less stratification among jobs and occupations than one would expect to find in the mechanical model in which the man at the top is always the same person in the same job.

The major distinction between our dynamic and static

styles and the Burns and Stalker organic and mechanical models is the different kinds of variables that have been used to characterize the two organizational systems. We have placed the emphasis on the characteristics that can be used to describe the social means and ends of the organization, which is more in the tradition of Max Weber. They have placed the emphasis on characteristics that can be used to describe the relationships between individuals in an organization, which is more in the tradition of Emile Durkheim. The terms "organic" and "mechanical" were used by Durkheim to describe two styles of societal integration. In a society with organic solidarity, integration is based on the functional interdependence of the division of labor, that is, the interdependence of many different occupational specialties. In a society with mechanical solidarity, integration is based on the common rules and norms of behavior. Burns and Stalker have applied these concepts and ideas of Durkheim to organizational life.

Because the essence of the Durkheimian approach is to focus on the relationship between individuals, many of the characteristics of the organic and mechanical models represent variables of communication or interaction. The content of communication is information and advice in an organic system, but instructions and decisions in a mechanical one. The former system has a high degree of horizontal interaction; the latter one has a high degree of vertical interaction. In an organic system, members are expected to be committed to organizational tasks and to the value of progress; in a mechanical system, members are expected to be loyal to the organization, to their superiors, and to tradition. The former system places an emphasis on general knowledge and experience; the latter places an emphasis on local knowledge and experience. In the organic organization, decisions are made in committees and in many informal meetings between department heads. There is a continuing shift in leadership, depending on the nature of the problem. Coordination is thus affected via continuous interaction of many specialists. In contrast, decisions are made by a few members of the elite in a mechanical organization. There is a "factory bible" that delineates what is usually to be done in most cases. There is not only less horizontal communication, that is, meetings among individuals on the same level of the hierarchy, but less communication in general. In conclusion, our two organizational styles not only represent two extremes along an organizational continuum, but they also differ in many other ways. We could add each of these dimensions to the configurations of the dynamic and static organization, but this would result in too complicated a discussion.

There is thus an inherent logic to both the static and the dynamic organizational models. No given organization is likely to fit one of these two types exactly. We would argue, however, that organizational mixtures of these characteristics are probably in a state of transition and that there is a tendency in the long run toward one of these two logical configurations. But under what circumstances does the organization tend toward the dynamic model and under what circumstances does an organization move toward the static style?

Causes of Change in Organizational Style

An understanding of the sources of change in organizational style requires us first to examine the relationship of the organization with its environment. We have previously defined the environment as anything external to the organization. In the case of a manufacturing firm, the environment includes the units that provide raw materials, banks, insurance companies, distributors, universities, or organizations that provide managerial talent, and so forth. In the case of welfare organizations, the environment includes local, state, and federal governmental units, the local community chest, other welfare organizations, and its clients.

Stable Environment and the Movement Toward a Static Style   If the relations between an organization and the environment reach some degree of stability; that is, if influences from the environment attain some degree of equilibrium, then we would argue that the organization is likely to move toward the static model. On the other hand, if relationships with the environment are more dynamic and if relationships with the environment are changing, then the organization is more likely to move toward the dynamic model. But this is only part of the story. Given static relationships with the environment, the organization is likely to become centralized. After this occurs, other characteristics of the static organization are likely to emerge. If the organization does not have static relations with the environment, then the forces inherent in diverse and highly professionalized occupational perspectives are likely to move the organization toward the dynamic style. Because these processes are rather complex, it is necessary to examine them in some depth.

The emergence of a static style can best be explained by examination of the "iron law of oligarchy." In a provocative book entitled *Political Parties,* Robert Michels argues that all organizations are inherently antidemocratic, or to use our terminology, organizations have a tendency to become centralized. His reasoning is as follows: Direct democracy, or maximal participation of all organizational members in making the decisions that dictate the policies of an organization is impossible for mechanical and technical reasons, especially as organizations increase in size. It is often imperative, however, that decisions be made quickly and decisively, thus limiting the number of organizational members who can play a part in decision making. Therefore, any organization must have an elite or leadership group, which of necessity is a minority of its members. Leadership is indispensable; and this leadership has control over the instrumentalities of the organization, that is, the finances, information, and mechanisms of administrative control such as rules and discipline. Autocratic, or centralizing, tendencies continually occur and leaders are likely to utilize those resources at their disposal in order to maintain themselves in power. Michels saw a strong tendency of this drift towards oligarchy as an organization increased in size.

What do we mean by a stable environment? If the organization has a continual growth in demand for its products or services and there are no major changes in the technology associated with the production of its products or services, then the environment is stable for the organization. There are other factors that can cause a change in the organization's environment. For example, the competitors may merge or the government may place certain restrictions on the organization, but in most cases these other factors will affect the demand for the products and/or services of the organization.

While Michels, who was studying political parties, a very special kind of organization, felt that size was the major factor accounting for the movement towards centralization, the stability of the environment facilitates this process in a number of ways. If the elite of an organization can safely predict that each year their growth in sales or their growth in clients will be about the same as the growth in the population, then it becomes possible to plan work schedules rationally. Most decisions can be made by a few individuals because there are so few occasions for making decisions. Based on years of experience, rules can be successfully written; and status differences will become sharp between the few who write the factory bible or the rules manual and the many who follow its dictates. In other words, a stable or predictable environment makes life easier for the organizational elite.

Burns and Stalker found that the Scottish companies which mass-produced vacuum tubes had a steady growth in sales year after year and approximated the mechanical model.[10] There were few crises in these firms and, therefore, little need for much decision making. Another study that supports Burns and Stalker is that of Stinchcombe, who found that mass-production industries in the United States were often highly centralized and low in complexity, relying primarily on unskilled labor.[11] In contrast, craft industries, such as construction in which demand was much less predictable and each product tended to be made to the specification of the customer, were more decentralized and had much greater complexity, relying on skilled labor.

To return to our own discussion, this tendency toward oligarchy or centralization is likely to take place under the conditions of an equilibrium between the organization and its environment. If this tendency toward centralization occurs, then the organization is likely to tend toward the static model for reasons developed previously in this discussion. In other words, we are suggesting that the trend toward centralization of organizational decision making is likely to occur first; and then there will be a tendency toward other organizational characteristics, such as high formalization, high stratification, and low complexity as well as toward development of policies reflecting efficiency, low morale, and high quantity of production.

Unstable Environment and the Movement Toward a Dynamic Style   The circumstances that lead to the static organizational model assume a stable relationship with the environment. But what happens if the relationship of the organization with the environment is in a state of flux? How can we explain the emergence of more dynamic organizations?

Perhaps the most important factor in the environment that leads to instability in an organization is the growth in knowledge. This can affect both the demand for products and/or services as well as the technology used in the manufacture of products or provision of services. The creation of the automobile forced many wagon manufacturers to either go out of business or to create new products. Studebaker used to make wagons before it became an automobile manufacturer. Declining sales for its automobiles finally forced it to go into entirely different lines of business. Similarly, the development of polio vaccine forced the National Infantile Paralysis Foundation to seek new types of clients.[12] These are dramatic examples, but to lesser degrees many organizations face an ever-changing environment that forces them to develop new programs and to add new occupations and skills. It is a question of survival.

To understand how fast the environment is changing, it is

necessary to understand the growth in research and development in the United States since the end of World War II. During the 1940s, research and development expenditures accounted for 2.5 percent of the gross national product (GNP) of the United States.[13] By the 1950s, this proportion had increased to 3.5 percent of the GNP. The government was contributing the greatest share of this, but private industry was also increasing its research activities. In 1960, private industry was spending some $4.6 billion per year on research and development. This had increased to $6.1 billion by 1965. Nor was all of this money just being spent on the development of new products. Basic research—research for the sake of knowledge—was becoming a steadily increasing share of the total amount of funds. Basic research increased 16 percent per year from 1953 through 1963. This growth in knowledge creates a changing environment for many organizations that provide products and services.

Unfortunately we do not know precisely in which areas knowledge has grown. The expenditures on research occur in some areas and not in others, so that not all organizations necessarily are confronted with a changing environment.

Another key to understanding the development of a dynamic style is in knowing the degree of complexity. Once complexity increases in an organization, the organization is less likely to become static. Again a changing environment forces an organization to become more complex and thus dynamic. As industrialized societies become more developed, the division of labor increases and new occupations and specializations are created. Greater knowledge about previously highly specific tasks occurs, and more and more highly trained personnel who are potential organizational members become available. Thus changes in the larger society create a pool of highly trained experts. Organizations that have a high diversity of occupational skills already are likely to have new programs continually suggested by these staffs. As decisions are made to proceed with a new program, organizations draw upon this external pool of highly trained experts. The consequence is that new programs in the organization require new types of professions or technically trained experts, who in turn feed new ideas and new demands for still other new programs. Thus these changes in the organizational environment permit the increase of occupational diversity and consequently an increase in the rate of program change.

In which kinds of organizations are there the greatest likelihood of hiring those trained in new occupations? It is in those organizations that have a concern with the quality of their product or service. If the members of a hospital are concerned about the quality of patient care, they will add new medical and paramedical specialties as they become available. Similarly, universities, research institutes, welfare agencies, mental hospitals, and so forth that are concerned with the quality of service will be likely to hire men with new occupational and organizational perspectives as they become available. Because knowledge is generally growing in the nation and because many new occupational specialties are being created, many organizations are becoming more complex, which will probably result in higher rates of program change.

Once a new program is created, the equilibrium of the organization will undoubtedly be upset. The relationship among ping-pong balls representing different organizational dimensions will be altered by the introduction of a new program, a new occupational perspective, or highly trained specialists. Thus, some new equilibrium among the organizational characteristics will have to occur. Highly trained organizational participants are likely to demand a greater part in organizational decision making. Therefore, the complexity of the organization introduces a tendency toward decentralization, and likewise toward less stratification and less formalization. The organizational policies characteristic of the dynamic organization—high morale, emphasis on quality, and so forth—are also likely to be emphasized in the newly evolved organizational form.

Another factor that can affect the complexity of an organization is a policy of expansion that involves diversification rather than horizontal or vertical integration. If a gunpowder company purchases a paint company, then it has increased its complexity because different skills are utilized in these two different kinds of technologies. Business firms that have followed a policy of diversification, for example, Du Pont, General Motors, or General Dynamics, have been forced to decentralize so as to make decisions more effectively.[14] Even a policy of horizontal integration can result in increased complexity if there are customers who make different demands on the organization. Thus, Sears, Roebuck and Company was forced to decentralize as it spread its stores across the country only to discover that different regions had different tastes.[15] In each instance organizational policy led to an increase in organizational complexity with the effect that the antidemocratic tendency of organizations was overcome. The consequences of antitrust laws have made horizontal and vertical integration difficult and have forced business firms with a considerable amount of money available for investment to diversify. In turn, this has increased the complexity of these organizations and has resulted in their becoming more dynamic.

Perhaps the most important factor in the environment, especially for business organizations, is the stability of the demand for services and products. If there is a steady, large demand for a product or service as in the case of railroads, telephone, cigarettes, food, steel, or copper, then the organizations providing these products are likely to be highly static. But if the demand is unsteady and unpredictable for a product or service, as in the case of chemicals, drugs, airplanes, electronics, or computers, then the organizations making these products are likely to be highly dynamic. Organizations that deal with continuously changing market conditions are forced to keep developing new products; this means a high rate of program change, which also means the eventual appearance of the other characteristics of a dynamic organizational style. Such organizations are likely to have large research and development activities that contribute to a high program change rate. Given the unstable relationship between the organization and its environment, such activities become neecssary for survival.

Some recent examples of this are the declining market for steel and the fear of a declining market for cigarettes, two industries that previously had large and stable demands. As steel companies lost more and more business to aluminum, glass, rubber, magnesium, and other industries during the 1950s, the response was to establish research departments.[16] These departments, representing an increase in occupational specialization, have developed many new products and thus have increased the rate of program change. For example, Lukens developed a new low-cost steel plate for low temperatures, Republic Steel created a vaporized aluminum coating for steel, Armco developed a new stainless steel, and the U.S. Steel Corporation announced that its research department was offering at least one new or improved product each month.[17] The crucial point is that once a company in an industry starts to develop new programs through research, it changes the environment of its competitors. The competitors must also develop new products or services with the consequence that change in the environment is accelerated. The organization's complexity increases, and the tendency toward a dynamic style is maintained.

Perhaps a much more interesting contemporary example of this phenomenon is the cigarette industry. For years, there was a steady and predictable demand for cigarettes. As the population grew, so did cigarette consumption. Then came the Surgeon General's report that suggested a link between cancer and smoking. In the first three months after the publication of the report, cigarette consumption was down 11 percent. In the second three months, after people had recovered somewhat from their scare, consumption was down only 6 percent. But the cigarette companies could no longer be sure about public response.[18] The government may eventually pass legislation affecting the demand for cigarettes. New York City increased the taxes on cigarettes, and publishers started distributing books on how to give up smoking. The cigarette companies responded with increased research to create a safe cigarette and a policy of product diversification—both resulting in greater complexity. For example, Liggett and Myers purchased a dog-food company and R. J. Reynolds bought a pineapple food-processing company. By the end of 1964, Phillip Morris was making 15 percent of its sales from nontobacco items, and P. Lorillard Co., had created a new job, Director of Corporate Planning and Development, a position designed to search for possible companies to purchase. The cigarette companies, faced with the prospect of declining demand because of the cancer scare, have responded by diversifying their products and purchasing other companies with different technologies.

Closely related to this is the duration of the demand for a particular product or service. As knowledge continually accelerates, as it has with the emphasis on research, the product life becomes shorter and shorter, forcing companies to allocate even more effort to research and development. An example of this is the chemical industry. Before World War II, Du Pont could manufacture a new product such as nylon and enjoy uninterrupted profits for twelve years. Now when it creates new products, there are two or three competitors with similar or better products almost immediately.[19] Du Pont manufactures some 1,200 products, and accounts for only 7 percent of all chemical sales in the United States. *The New York Times* has described this situation in the chemical industry as one in which "new products are boiling up daily."[20] Such rapid changes in the environment as these are likely to prevent a company from moving toward the static style. Another example is in the drug industry in which some 500 new products are manufactured each year. As a consequence, most drugs can be expected to have a market for only a few years before a better drug is developed. It goes without saying that if a company tailor-makes its products, as do some organizations, there is likely to be a very short-term demand. As Burns and Stalker suggest, such companies must have a dynamic style.

Most of these examples are of business firms. Can the same thing be said for nonprofit organizations, such as hospitals, schools, research institutes, or welfare agencies? We would answer in the affirmative. Growth in knowledge creates a changing environment for these organizations as well. In fact, much of the growth in knowledge takes place in universities or research institutes, organizations that are already complex. In our own research, we found most of the sixteen welfare organizations to be moving toward the dynamic style.

There is still another way in which occupational diversity is likely to trigger the process that eventually results in a more dynamic organization. Often it is quite expensive to introduce new programs and techniques in an organization. One solution is the creation of a joint activity or joint program with some other organization. The joint program is likely to permit program change at a reduced cost for each participating organization. But as this is done with many organizations, the dynamic organizations become involved in a wide network of interorganizational relationships. At first one may infer that this increase in organizational interdependence and seeming decrease in organizational autonomy might restrict the organization's propensity towards greater change. What happens is just the opposite. Organizations involved in many joint programs take on "high visibility" in the community. The greater professionalism and consequently the higher quality of services gain even greater attention in the "organizational community."

At least four consequences of this greater interorganizational involvement are likely to occur. First, the increased contact with other organizations is likely to lead to increased knowledge in the organization; insights on how to do existing jobs even better may be the consequences of these joint ventures. There may be an increase in professional standards. Second, the involvement with other organizations is likely to present serious problems of coordination for the organization. The fact that commitments to other organizations place restraints upon rules and procedures means that the organization is likely to have a series of short-run "organizational fires" to put out. The answer is more committee meetings and other such communicative activities within the organization. Translated into organizational jargon, this means heightened internal communication. Communication up and down the chain of command (vertical) and across departments (horizontal) must be increased. Third, the increased visibility as well as the increased pace of communication in the organization are likely to lead to higher organizational morale. Organizational members are not only likely to receive acknowledgement from the outside world for their accomplishments, but also from inside the organization. The increased communication is also likely to spill over into organizational problems not necessarily directly related to the joint organizational programs that initiated it. In other words, the necessity of greater internal coordination because of these external constraints "oils the organizational machinery." The increased communication activities mean greater participation in decision making, that is, greater organizational decentralization. And finally, such joint programs and activities may result in the introduction of new occupational specialties to the organization, perhaps only on a part-time basis. The long-run consequence of this is to feed the very process that started it; that is, increased occupational diversity and heightened professionalism are likely to contribute to the growth of additional joint programs and activities, thus leading not to the seeds of their own destruction, to paraphrase Marx, but to new joint programs and the seeds of their own creation. These comments, together with our earlier comments about formalization, stratification, efficiency, and productivity provide still another rationale for the processes that move organizations toward the dynamic style.

We have argued that the variable of complexity is likely to be the triggering mechanism that leads to the dynamic organizational model. But given stable and nonchanging relationships between the organization and its environment, then the dynamics described here will less likely occur. Under such static circumstances the "iron law of oligarchy," or centralization, and eventually the static organization, is likely to emerge.

But given conditions other than a static equilibrium between the organization and its environment, the process that grows out of organizational complexity is likely to occur.

Obviously reality is never so cut and dried as our description here. There may be in a short period of time rapid fluctuations in environmental conditions. This, of course, complicates the organizational process because a tendency toward decentralization may have begun only to be disrupted by a market decline for the business firm, increased students for the educational institution, the discovery of a new treatment by the health or social welfare organization, or a new law for the governmental agency. In such an event there would be a countervailing tendency towards the dynamic style. Rather than arguing about the delicate balances of reality, we are more interested in suggesting the energizing sources that push organizations toward either the dynamic or static model.

Case Histories of Changing Styles

When an organization alters one of its basic characteristics —for example, it moves from high to low centralization—other characteristics alter as well. This can be observed in several case histories of organizations. The hypotheses that we have suggested have not been explicitly used in any studies, but many of the eight organizational characteristics have been included in the descriptions of organizations that have changed their rate of program change. It, therefore, becomes possible to test the idea that the eight characteristics form a social system of interrelated variables instead of just assuming that it does.

Although a university, a chemical company, a prison, a hospital, and an advertising agency have different objectives, at the same time the decision makers face similar organizational problems about which they must formulate policies.

Case of a College During the middle of the nineteenth century, American colleges faced a continual decline in enrollment.[21] At the same time the proportion of the population attending college was increasing. More and more Americans were going to Europe to study. A large number of these were attending the new German universities, such as the University of Berlin, in which it was possible to study any one of a number of the new sciences. In other words, American colleges were not competing effectively. The demand for their services was declining. This had not gone unnoticed, having been mentioned in a speech by the president of Brown as early as the 1850s. But the resistance was so great to the new sciences among the existing faculties of American colleges that it was difficult to introduce these new occupational specialties into American universities.

Shortly after the end of the Civil War in the United States, Harvard needed a new president. At this time Harvard had not suffered as much as the other New England colleges; its enrollments were keeping pace with the growth in population. The selection of James Eliot, the first president who was not a clergyman, represented a sharp break with the past. He had studied science and, at the time of his selection, was teaching chemistry at a newly founded college, Massachusetts Institute of Technology. Eliot was young, only thirty-five at the time. Whether these were factors important for Eliot's selection by the Harvard board is hard to say. But the fact that Eliot had an entirely different career sequence meant that he came to Harvard with a different perspective from many of his new colleagues.

Within the first few years Eliot introduced a series of changes. The most important, from our perspective, were those that resulted in radical changes in organizational complexity. He doubled the size of the faculty, hiring mostly young men trained in new academic disciplines. Instead of relying on the existing faculty to make recommendations, Eliot went out of his way to secure men with different intellectual perspectives. He introduced not only men of the new sciences but also men in the new social sciences such as economics.

The power structure of Harvard was altered in several ways

by Eliot. He created the new position of dean and delegated considerable authority to him. Eliot attended faculty meetings and increased the number of these meetings, with many complaints being registered by the old faculty. If Eliot met resistance to a particular idea, he would let the matter rest and bring it up again at a later date. In these meetings, the majority vote counted. Thus there was decentralization of decision making.

A number of student regulations were eliminated: The rules manual was reduced from forty pages to five; compulsory chapel was eliminated; perhaps the most dramatic change was the abolishing of the fixed curriculum instruction. Gradually the concept of electives was introduced into American education.

It would be easy to see these changes as a consequence of Eliot's leadership, and this certainly was an important factor in bringing about the radical alteration in the social structure of Harvard. But it is important to recognize that what Eliot did was to increase the complexity of the organization and to decentralize its structure. Once new occupational specialties were brought in, new ideas were generated by the men in these specialties. Gradually research laboratories were introduced. The new dean of the law school and his faculty introduced the famous case method, which later became the method for most law schools in the United States. And finally the medical school curriculum was revised. Once Eliot had increased the complexity of the college, the development of new programs continued of its own accord. These new programs gradually led to the development of a graduate school in 1890. And thus Harvard became Harvard University.

There was an important environmental factor that facilitated the introduction of new programs: the competition between universities for good men. During the period of Eliot's forty years as president of Harvard, two new universities—Johns Hopkins and the University of Chicago—were created. These new universities attempted to hire leading faculty members away from Harvard. When men received offers from other schools, they used this as a bargaining device to support the implementation of their new ideas. A Harvard man, after receiving an offer from Johns Hopkins, obtained research support that later led to his winning a Nobel Prize. Thus the competition between organizations helps maintain a high rate of program change in a complex organization.

Case of a Chemical Company   During World War I, the management of Du Pont, largely a manufacturer of explosives at the time, recognized that after the war it would have large unused plant facilities and large profits to invest.[22] The executive committee decided it would be advantageous to invest in chemical products in the United States since Germany had lost its market in this country and there was not much existing competition. Du Pont started buying chemical plants and manufacturers of paints, dyes, and rubber coatings. After the war, Du Pont began to experience difficulties with its policy of product diversification. Most of these new products were resulting in losses, even though competitors were making profits. A subcommittee was appointed to recommend what should be done about the situation. The members, all young, professionally trained, and experienced managers, recommended creating a general manager for each major product line who would have authority for making sales, purchasing, and accounting decisions as well as authority over production and distribution. The report was rejected by the president. He felt that the organization needed more information, not decentralization.

By 1921, Du Pont was plunged into the middle of a financial crisis. On the recommendation of a manager, the president and the executive committee decided to decentralize and to create a long-term planning committee. This led not only to decentralization, but also to the creation of specialized procedures for each of the different products. The chief of purchasing attempted to retain centralization of decision making in this area; however, power was gradually decentralized here too.

The case of Du Pont, unlike Harvard, is a case in which the changes in organization were not brought about by the president, but by a crisis that forced the president to go along with the recommendations of his managerial staff. But like the Harvard example, it illustrates the organization's operating as a system. Du Pont tried to have high complexity with high centralization, but this situation proved to be too inflexible to meet the different market demands on the organization. The decentralized structure of Du Pont is still in existence today. In the intervening years, Du Pont continuously developed many new products, none of which was the idea of any single leader, but the result of ideas from many different sources. In fact, Du Pont has had one of the largest and most successful research efforts—efforts that have contributed to a high rate of program change in the organization.

Case of a Prison   McCleery's study of a prison represents even less planning of change than occurred in the chemical company.[23] This study illustrates how the hiring of men outside of the organization can produce changes internally and how changes in the general society, that is, the development of new occupational specialties, can have an effect on organizations. The seeds of the first change occurred with the replacement of five men from 1946 to 1949. Each of these men came from outside the prison; and having no previous experience in the organization, they brought with them different values and perspectives. McCleery points out that the prison had made no explicit change in recruitment policy, which means that the consequences of this change in recruitment pattern was unanticipated.

It is necessary to describe the actual organizational structure of the prison prior to the changes. The prison was very much like the static organization described at the end of Chapter 2. Power was largely centralized in the positions of Warden and Deputy Warden; only these two men made policy decisions. There was a strict hierarchy of authority and tight discipline. Labor in work groups was viewed as a mechanism of control rather than an opportunity for training. Sharp class distinctions among prison convicts were maintained. Ideas for improvement were repressed. Work supervisors came to think, act, and dress like guards. There was an absence of two-way communications—all communication flowed downward. A high degree of discipline was maintained while applying few direct sanctions; and social control was created through constant regimentation and supervision. There were frequent counts and assemblies. Parallel to the formal hierarchy of the prison employees, there was also a hierarchy among the prisoners. Here, too, there was a small elite that maintained strict control and sharp status differences.

The new men began to place an emphasis on open communication between levels, on justice rather than on a concern for control, and on performance in work groups rather than on conformity. By-passing the official channels, they discussed their ideas directly with the warden. The warden listened to their ideas, and gradually the new men became policy makers. A new organization chart was made, placing the new men's departments on the same level as the guard force. A policy committee was created in which the guards, who constituted the largest department, were underrepresented and outnumbered. Thus power became decentralized and was formalized in a new policy manual which stated:

> The delegation to lower management levels of all possible responsibility and authority commensurate with sound management. A practice of constant consultation, dissemination of information, and discussion of problems up and down the management chain.

Gradually a number of rules and procedures of regimentation were abolished. The time-honored salute in all contacts between inmates and guards was eliminated, status differences between work supervisors and inmates were reduced, and a series of inmates committees were created to develop programs in the areas of food, hobbies, craft work, education, recreation, and public relations. All of these changes resulted in flattening the status and authority pyramids and narrowing the gaps of social distance.

Case of a Hospital   During the 1950s, a shortage of internship positions developed in community hospitals. In an effort to compete more effectively, some community hospitals began to add a new occupational specialty, the director of medical education, to its structure.[24] Originally the purpose of this new position was to recruit interns and to develop a more extensive medical education program. One community hospital that was having difficulty in recruiting interns hired as their director of medical education (D.M.E.), a man who had been trained in university hospitals and had, as a consequence, a different set of standards concerning quality of education and patient care. Thus declining demand by interns for the available positions—the equivalent to product demand—forced the organization to add a new specialty.

The new D.M.E., Dr. Bacon, developed a plan for improving the social performances in the community hospital. By gaining foundation support, he was able to hire a number of new physicians. These new men provided a number of new skills for the hospital; the occupational specialties included full-time teachers for each of the major clinical services and hematology, neurology, endocrinology, cardiology, and infectious diseases, a series of medical subspecialties not previously represented in the hospital. These men started adding a series of new programs and developing existing services. Teaching ward service was added, teaching rounds in each of the medical subspecialties were developed, grand rounds for each clinical service were either increased in frequency or made more effective, special laboratory tests were provided, and several research studies were started.

As a consequence of the initiation and implementation of these programs, a series of power conflicts developed in the hospital. Gradually these conflicts, particularly those between the new physicians and the older physicians on the active staff, resulted in a decentralization of the power structure. The power of the administration increased as did that of the new physicians, the interns, and the residents. The creation of a department of medical education and the initiation of weekly meetings resulted in the establishment of new communication links between the various departments and services of the hospital.

This study represents an interesting contrast to the prison study. There conflicts developed after moving the power structure toward decentralization. In the case of the community hospital, the power structure altered as a result of the conflicts, particularly those involving the addition of new programs or services. However, both of these studies involve examples of how changes were introduced because of new recruitment patterns. They also represent a contrast to the study of Harvard and Du Pont because the newly recruited men were not powerful, at least not at the outset. In particular, there was little support from the leadership of the hospital; new programs and services were thus introduced at a much slower rate than they were in the prison in which the warden was sympathetic to the increased emphasis on treatment.

Both the quality of medical education and of patient care improved. The caliber of interns and residents, as reflected by the medical schools from which they graduated, increased. The hospital was able to attract almost a full quota of American-trained interns—a phenomenon rare for a community hospital —and especially considering its location.

The cost of operating the hospital increased, although this was not only a result of the increased payroll necessitated by the added full-time teachers and supporting personnel. The number of lab tests ordered increased 25 percent, reflecting increased availability and increased quality of patient care. In many other areas of hospital operation, there were increased costs as well.

The rate of program change of the hospital grew in areas other than the medical area. The addition of new medical occupations resulted in an increased awareness of the need for changes in all areas of the hospital. The consequence of this self-examination was the addition of new programs and techniques in other departments, a reshuffling of personnel in key positions, a reallocation of the budget, and still more new occupations such as public relations.

The hospital altered from a static to a dynamic style, from a concern about the number of patients handled to a concern about the quality of patient handling, from mechanical integration toward the organic form of interdependence.

Case of an Advertising Agency   The four previous cases have represented illustrations of the addition of new occupations and programs and the movement from a static to a dynamic style. In each organization, the increase in occupations, one indication of the magnitude of the change, was great. It is entirely possible for an organization to move in the opposite direction, however, from a dynamic to a static style. In this situation, occupations are not subtracted as much as there is a general tightening of the organizational chain of command, the breaking of communication lines, and the standardization of procedures.

The reason for the change in the advertising agency was the loss of several major accounts.[25] The leadership of the agency decided that it had to create tighter control over each of its accounts so that there would be more effective service. This policy was reflected in the centralization of power in the hands of the account executives. Whereas previously each of the major occupational specialties in advertising such as copywriters, layout men, and media specialists had their own departments, these were disbanded under the reorganization. A specific person in each occupational specialty was assigned to a specific account, under the supervision of the account executive.

This change precipitated other changes. Procedures became more formalized. Interaction between the professionals of a particular occupational specialty decreased, that is, interaction became largely vertical. Morale went down and many individuals quit their jobs. Kover reported that there were two types of ad men: the careerists and the craftsmen. The former were concerned with promotions and status differences; the latter, with the quality of their work. It was the craftsmen who suffered the greatest loss of morale and left the agency. Efficiency under the new structure increased, suggesting again the fact that an organization is a system of interrelated variables.

Conclusions

In this chapter, we have begun to introduce further complexities into our discussion of social change in complex organizations. We have introduced additional reasons as to why the eight variables or dimensions defined in Chapter 1 are interrelated. Not only are complexity and centralization related to the rate of program change, but also these two variables are themselves related. We have introduced other dimensions, suggesting that these too are part of the organizational system. Finally, we have related the characteristics of the environment and its alterations to organizational change. Thus our analysis of social change has attempted to link external and internal change together into a coherent chain of events. Now it is necessary to consider in some detail the process of change, which is the topic of the next chapter.

4 Stages and Strategies: The Problem of the Change Process

So far we have examined organizational change from a relatively static point of view. For example, we have related organizational and environmental characteristics to the rate of change in organizations, but we have not examined the process of social change; that is, we have not examined the actual sequence of events over time that are involved in any alteration of organizational structures. Such an examination makes social change in organizations much more real to us.

It will be helpful to divide the time sequence of the process of organizational change into four periods or stages. The first, *evaluation*, is a period of study and assessment of the need for a new program. The second and third stages, *initiation* and *implementation*, were introduced in Chapter 2. The fourth stage, *routinization*, is a period in which the organization attempts to stabilize the effects of the new program; unfortunately, this stage has received too little attention in various studies of organizations.

Each stage presents organizational decision makers with crucial organizational problems that must be solved. Although these stages are rather artificial in one sense, that is, the end of one stage may not be clearly distinguishable from the beginning of another stage, they are still useful analytical categories to assist in understanding the process of change. These stages are discussed in the first section of this chapter.

There have been even fewer studies of the pattern of change than of its causes and consequences. Therefore, there are not adequate illustrations of the problems involved in each stage. In the second section of this chapter, a detailed discussion of social change in a hospital illustrates how these analytical categories may be used to describe the process of change.

In the third and final section of this chapter, we shall examine other approaches that describe the stages of organizational change. Specifically, we shall examine three other works: a discussion of individual acceptance of innovation, a study of social change during the Industrial Revolution in Britain, and a study of social change in complex organizations. In each instance we shall compare these works with our own conceptualization of the phases or stages in the process of social change.

Stages in the Process of Organizational Change

We have argued that organizations are highly interdependent entities. That is, our analogy of the ping-pong balls emphasizes the idea that a change in one part of a social system affects another part of that system, but these changes do not occur instantaneously throughout all parts of an organization. The impact of change in an organization spreads gradually. This is the reason for trying to understand the process of change by defining a series of stages.

Interdependence is by no means a new idea. Economists have long discussed how the economy of a nation is a system and that changes in one part of that system, such as a change in the interest rate, may have an effect on the rate of investment; this in turn may ultimately affect the rate of unemployment. Such changes do not necessarily occur in a mechanical way, however. If the interest rate increases by 1 percent, the rate of investment may decline by 5 percent the first month, 15 percent the second month, and so forth. Similarly, the unemployment rate may also be affected by a mathematical function that changes over time. In other words, the relationship is not linear. In our discussion of organizations we envisage changes occurring in an analogous manner. The way we represent this change is through the discussion of four stages: evaluation, initiation, implementation, and routinization.

Evaluation Stage   The beginning of the process of organizational change occurs when organizational decision makers determine that either the organization is not accomplishing its present goals as effectively or efficiently as possible or when decision makers alter or amend the goals of the organization. In the former case the decision to make a change may result from a study of various aspects of organizational performance: the volume of production, the efficiency of production, or the morale of organizational members. Many organizations make periodic evaluations of organizational performances—annual profit statements, annual reports, or perhaps annual job evaluations. If this periodic report indicates that the organization has failed to attain one of its objectives, the elite may decide it is time for a change. Sometimes failure occurs dramatically as in the case of a manufacturer having declining sales for a major product. The steel, coal, and railroad companies have experienced this problem during the past two decades. Sometimes failure occurs gradually and is only recognized after a period of time. For example, declining enrollments in a college or decreasing clients in a welfare agency may be attributed to factors that do not have their origin in the organization.

During the evaluation stage decision makers must assess the state of health of an organization, consider alternative ways of correcting organizational problems, and then decide on one alternative that hopefully will accomplish the desired ends. The decision about the future course of the organization predisposes the organization to the second stage, the actual initiation of a new activity, whether a service or product.

What kinds of organizations are likely to have continual evaluation procedures? The organization that is concerned with the quality of its service or product is most likely to appraise its success or failure continually and to attempt to improve its performance. As we have argued in the previous chapter, there is an inherent dynamism in an organization with a high degree of complexity, especially if policy is oriented to improving the quality of product or service. As prospective members receive longer and longer periods of training, they are concerned more and more with a standard of excellence, which requires constant evaluation of the organization.

One result of continued evaluation is the increased possibility that value conflicts will arise. People are likely to differ over which standards they apply in evaluating the effectiveness of the organization. Many of the current conflicts between students, administration, and faculty in large universities reflect value conflicts about the proper role of the university. Each of these groups is likely to use different criteria in evaluating the success or failure of the organization. Students consider the accessibility of the professor and the caliber of his lectures to be most important; whereas, faculty members may consider the support of the university in their research activities to be the crucial factor in determining the success of the university. The administration may use still different criteria such as the size of the research budget or the number of students graduated as the best indicators of the university's effectiveness.

Closely connected to the problem of differences of opinion

about which criteria should be used in assessing the relative success or failure of the organization is the choice of the particular solution to improve the performance of the organization. Different occupational groups may have different solutions for the problem, and this may create additional conflicts. But such conflicts are about the means to solve problems, not organizational ends.

In the choice of a solution the organization faces a dilemma. On the one hand, the organization can decide to be cautious and choose a modest change that does not depart noticeably from the previous product, service, or activity of the organization. On the other hand, the organization can attempt to solve its problem by a solution that represents a radical departure from previous organizational activities. The disadvantage of the former strategy is that the change may not solve the problem, but the disadvantage of the latter strategy is that the risk may be too great and threaten the continued existence of the organization. The greater the scope of a new program being considered, the more acute these problems become. There is an inevitable gamble in the development of any new activity. The elite of an organization may perceive that the change will meet the needs of their customers or clients, but it may not in fact. Therefore, the elite must decide how innovative they want to be when selecting a solution for the improvement of organization performances.

Initiation Stage   When the decision makers of an organization have decided to add a new program or activity to the organization—whether it be a new product in a business firm, a new social service in a health or welfare organization, or a new course of instruction in a school—it often reflects long, arduous hours of thought and deliberation about the appropriateness of this particular solution for the organizational problem. But the decision of a given alternative is likely to start a chain reaction, triggering other organizational problems. This occurs because organizations are such highly interdependent entities; a change in one part is likely to ramify eventually throughout the organization. Thus, problems of adjustment among departments or segments of an organization are likely to occur.

One of the first problems that an organization faces, once a decision has been made to add a program or activity, is to find prospective job occupants with the requisite skills and training to fill the occupational slots created by the addition of the new program. If the change involves the addition of a specialized physical therapy service in a rehabilitation agency, then one of the major problems at this stage is to find job occupants who can perform the physical therapy activity involved. Similarly, if the decision is to create a new line of hosiery in a garment manufacturing plant, the management must find staff and production personnel with adequate training and experience to implement the new product line.

There are two choices open to the decision makers. They can either recruit job occupants from outside the organization or else select individuals from inside the organization, that is, from their own staff. The more radical the new program as viewed from the previous history of the organization, the more organizational decision makers will probably have to rely on external recruitment. But this creates other problems. Bringing in strangers to implement a new program increases the likelihood of resistance to innovation by staff members already in the organization. On the other hand, if decision makers recruit internally, they are likely to select individuals who may be unaware of the full potentialities of the new program. The longer job occupants remain in an organization, the more they tend to develop a particular, and sometimes limited, point of view that can seriously mitigate the extent of the proposed change and thereby limit the amelioration of the organizational problem that led to the decision to innovate. The elite is thus faced with another dilemma: whether to recruit inside or outside the organization.

The seriousness of this dilemma can be ascertained by noting how many new occupations must be added to implement the new program. The more advanced the knowledge involved in the activity and the greater the number of different occupations that are to be involved, the greater the stimulus the new program may have for the organization. Consider the many new jobs created by the addition of a computer installation to a university or a manufacturing establishment. Programmers, key punch operators, mathematicians, and a host of other specialists may become necessary. The number of new occupations to be added provides a measure of the magnitude of the change and, therefore, the seriousness of the dilemma.

Another aspect of the initiation stage is the search for financial support for the new program. For many profit-making organizations, this may not be a problem because these organizations can support the programs out of operating funds. At the same time, even the largest company can have difficulties, depending upon the cost of the new product or service. When International Business Machines decided to launch its new 360 series of computers (even though it was still making profits on the old line), it required capitalization of almost five billion dollars, an amount equal to the entire worth of the company. In fact, the executives of the company referred to it as a new game: "Bet a corporation." [1]

The crucial problem faced in finding new programs is that financing sought from outside the organization may only be temporary and may result in some loss of control. On the other hand, if the financing is done within the organization, part of another program or activity may have to be curtailed because of the scarcity of funds. Again the organization may face a dilemma. It is this dilemma of financing that results in some organizations becoming involved in joint programs, thereby sharing the costs involved. But in the process they may lose some autonomy.

Perhaps the clearest example of a loss of autonomy was the formation of a joint fund-raising organization by the Baptist Church.[2] The purpose was to reduce the cost of fund raising for local churches, but another consequence was the gradual assumption of power by the new organization. Prior to the formation of the Baptist Convention, there had been a number of independent church organizations, each of which raised its own money. The formation of these many autonomous units reflected the basic Baptist commitment to democracy and the idea of a free church. The Baptists had originally formed as a reaction against the centralizing tendencies of some protestant churches, so the Baptist Convention was created in the United States as a device to create more effective and efficient services. Although a number of safeguards had been built into the convention's constitution, gradually the executive secretaries began to assume more and more power through the manipulation of church funds.

The question of the loss of autonomy via outside financing is part of the present criticism of federally sponsored programs. The large sums made available by the federal government provide a needed resource for the development of new programs, especially in health, education, and welfare, but some people have charged that the federal government is gaining control over the way the programs are to be run. The same problem occurs with financing by banks. Banks frequently insist on a series of safeguards that mean some control over the nature and content of the new program. This, of course, means some loss of autonomy by the organization.

A related aspect of this problem is the future financing of a new activity. Although an organizational elite may be able to support a more radical new approach with the help of outside financing, such sources of funds are likely to be temporary. Therefore, the elite must have some alternative source of support if a decision is made to retain the program during the routinization stage. A common complaint made by executive directors of welfare agencies is that the support of the federal government is frequently temporary and that alternative sources of support are not available once the federal funds are removed. Thus the seeking of outside funds is at best a temporary solution to the dilemma and may result in some loss of autonomy.

Implementation Stage   Perhaps the most interesting stage in the process of organizational change is the implementation stage because disequilibrium of the organization is greatest at this time. Certainly there are conflicts during the previous stages of change—we have already mentioned the value conflicts during the evaluation stage—but more members of the organization are likely to become involved in conflicts during the implementation stage. The previous two stages normally involve only the elite of the organization. The leaders, not the lower participants, decide whether the organization is experiencing success or failure, whether a new program is to be started or not, and what sources of people and funds are to be used.

Another reason that a new program is more likely to upset the equilibrium of an organization during the implementation stage than during previous stages is simply that during the implementation stage the program becomes a reality. In the previous two stages, the program exists only in theory. In that case, the prospect of a new program meeting the needs of customers or clients works well. It is during the implementation stage that these ideas must confront reality.

But the most important reason for the disequilibrium of the organization during this phase is that no matter how much the elite may plan, a plan is unlikely to consider all the potential sources of discontinuity between the new program and the existing organizational structure. Organizations can have operations researchers carefully design a system for handling a new program, but the human element is seldom adequately considered in the implementation of a new product or service. There will be mistakes that will have to be corrected. Alteration of the existing structure will also create conflicts and tensions among the members of the organization.

Why should the addition of a new program create conflict? Frequently the addition of a new activity means the creation of new social positions in the organization. The occupants of these new positions will fight for power, for the right to make rules, and for a share of the rewards in the organization. This does not mean that the new job occupants will say that they want more power and higher prestige. As Burns and Stalker note, the requests are always phrased in terms of what is good for the development of the program.[3] The new job occupants will want more authority in order to establish their new activity successfully. They will ask for the right to alter existing organizational rules in order to eliminate some of the discontinuities between the new program and its articulation with the existing structure. They will demand more space and other resources with the plea that these are needed if the activity is to be a success.

These requests create a dilemma for the organizational elite. Acceding to the demands may help the implementation of the new program, but it will also result in the alteration of the existing power structure. The reallocation of power will of course be resisted by the other job occupants whose influence may be decreased. If the elite do not accede to the demands, the new program may die, strangled by the rigidities of the existing structure.

Another factor making the implementation stage difficult is that frequently the success of a new program requires the active cooperation of other members of the organization. The broader the scope of the new venture, the more likely this is to be the case. If the lower participants do not cooperate, the program can be largely defeated by the passive or even active resistance of those members concerned with the actual operation of it. An excellent illustration was a series of new policies implemented by the Cooperative Commonwealth Federation party in Canada. The members lower in the chain of command of the government agencies did not cooperate, and many programs either were never begun or were established with only partial success.[4]

The gaining of active cooperation upon the part of the lower participants involved in the implementation of a program can be achieved by sharing the power of decision making with them.[5] But again a dilemma is created. If the lower participants share in the decision making, the plan may be curtailed by their diffuse and irrelevant suggestions. If the lower participants do not share in the decision making, the plan may be curtailed by their resistance. In either case, the implementation of the new program becomes problematical.

The history of the addition of therapeutic patient care to a mental hospital provides an illustration.[6] The chief of staff and the administration were wholeheartedly in favor of this innovation, but the psychiatrists, nurses, attendants, and some others had to alter their behavior toward the patient if the program was to be a success. In other words, the written job descriptions of many jobs had to be altered. Since these specialists were most intimately involved with the innovation, they were in a position to sabotage the new program, subtly if they so desired. The introduction of a therapeutic perspective into a traditionally custodial mental hospital is perhaps a dramatic case of some problems encountered during the implementation stage. The same principles apply to other types of innovations. The number of existing occupational incumbents whose behavior has to be altered in order to innovate provides some measure of the magnitude of change, and, therefore, the seriousness of the dilemma faced by organizational decision makers. In this particular instance, the decision making was shared. The nurses, attendants, and social workers were involved in the planning and implementation of the new program. As a consequence the program was successfully established.

Another problem associated with the implementation of a new program is that the program may be a good idea on paper, but that the planning will not have accounted for every contingency in the program. As a consequence, the innovation will have to be altered as it is established. This situation will create a continual strain on the interpersonal and interpositional relationships connected with the new activity, which is likely to become manifested in some form of social conflict. To make matters worse, unless the innovation is in a separate location—totally isolated from the existing activities of the organization—other programs may have to be altered. Seldom are all of these consequences anticipated, a fact that will also result in conflicts as the existing routine is disrupted and changed. It is for all these reasons that the equilibrium of an organization is disturbed and that the participants in a new program experience change as arduous and difficult.

An excellent example is the prison study by McCleery reported in the previous chapter.[7] As the rehabilitators increased their power, the guards inevitably lost power. The guards eventually rebelled against the loss of power and attempted to gain the support of members of the state legislature. The state legislature eventually started an official investigation of the prison. The proposed reforms were designed to bring about more humanitarian conditions for inmates; however, the legislative investigating committee supported the warden. This study suggests how a severe conflict may even result in third parties entering into the dispute. In this particular study, the decision making was not shared with the guards, and the consequence was a series of conflicts and active resistance.

Perhaps the simplest illustration of the problem of sharing decision making is the experience of Eliot at Harvard, one of the case studies reported in the previous chapter. He discussed each plan he had decided to implement with his faculty members; but frequently the faculty would vote against the plans. His usual reaction was to attempt to implement a new program in another college of the developing university. Fortunately for Harvard, Eliot was president for over forty years, so that eventually most of his ideas and those of others who advocated change prevailed and were eventually introduced.[8]

A similar situation was faced by Burgess at Columbia College before it became a university.[9] He asked the faculty to vote in favor of some new courses in political science that he wanted to teach. Although the faculty allowed the addition of the new courses, they stipulated that the courses were to be taught in hours other than those usually reserved for Columbia College students, thereby, hoping to defeat his proposal. When Burgess attempted to get the librarian to order new books for his courses, the librarian refused. This man also refused to allow the library to be open more than two hours a day. Finally, Burgess went to the Board of Regents and obtained permission to start an entirely new library.

Again, the elite of an organization face a dilemma between maximizing change and minimizing resistance. If they share power with lower participants to a great extent and use human relations techniques, the active cooperation of the lower participants is much more likely. However, there is a danger that the plan may be altered considerably as a result. If the elite do not share power, they may increase the intensity of the power, rule, and status conflicts that occur as the new program is implemented. The stage of implementation is thus the stage of conflict, especially over power. It is the time when the new program results in the greatest disequilibrium in the organization because it is the stage when the program becomes reality and the members of the organization must actually live with it. The problems and prospects of the innovation become much more apparent. Other programs are altered, tempers flare, interpersonal animosities develop, and the power structure is shaken. Whether the new program survives or dies, whether the power structure is altered or remains the same, there is the fourth stage—routinization—during which the organization attempts to achieve a new equilibrium.

Routinization Stage At some point the elite of an organization must decide whether or not the new program is meeting the organizational need for which it was designed. Because almost no studies have focused on this stage, it is difficult to specify reasons that some programs are retained and others are allowed to die. It is entirely possible that a new program may meet an organizational need, proving effective for the customers or clients of the organization, but that the elite may decide not to institutionalize the activity. If there has been too much conflict in the implementation stage, the elite may feel that the cure is worse than the disease. Further, the cost of financing the program may be too great in comparison to the gains obtained from it. But perhaps most importantly, the elite may not have sufficient objective measures of the success or failure of the innovation. Under such circumstances, the conflicts and difficulties created by the new program which are likely to be quite evident, may decide the issue. The lack of means to measure success or failure raises a basic problem that is in need of much more research and that has many implications for understanding how organizations move toward the dynamic style. The more the criteria include measures of quality, the more likely the new program is to be retained even though it will be recognized simultaneously that it has failings. The more the criteria include measures of efficiency, the more likely the new program might be rejected. If the elite's criteria of success or failure of the new program can be stipulated, then some prediction about the likelihood of the retention of an innovation is possible.

Regardless of the criteria used, at some point the elite must make a decision either to retain or reject the new program. If they decide to keep the innovation, a period of consolidation is begun. What was a new activity becomes integrated into the existing structure. If the innovation is abandoned, the organizational structure may revert to the pattern that existed prior to the initiation stage. If the program is continued, rules and regulations must be developed, which may not only include the writing of a rules manual but perhaps a detailed job description for each of the new positions involved in the new activity. The decision to standardize a program marks the beginning of the routinization stage.

This decision to integrate the new activity into the structure of the organization creates another dilemma for the elite. Does the decision come too soon or too late? Precisely because the new program cannot be completely planned in advance, there must be a time of trial and error for the innovation, a period in which the program is adjusted, altered, or modified as the personnel associated with the new activity attempt to make it work. There is some probability that the longer the elite allow this period of trial and error to continue, the greater the chances of the new program achieving its intended objectives. At the same time, this period is costly; and the conflicts engendered will encourage the elite to routinize the program into the existing structure as soon as possible. The question of when to institutionalize the new program becomes especially problematical if the effects of the program are long term. Long term evaluation periods make the question of success or failure particularly difficult to decide.

Closely related to the problem of establishing rules and procedures for the program is the problem of defining a proper role for the new program in the existing structure. The positions associated with the program must be fitted into the existing power structure and reward system. The program must be articulated with other programs, which means establishing definite procedures and policies in order to articulate these activities with other parts of the organization. The stabilization of the power and reward structures tends to result in the diminution of internal conflicts. Every occupant of a position now knows his place in the organizational chart, so that much of the ambiguity of the implementation stage has been resolved.

Perhaps the best sign of the routinization of the new program occurs when the men who were originally involved in implementing the program are replaced. If the program remains essentially the same, that is, it does not trigger another process of change, we can then say that it has been stabilized. Another sign of its routinization is the development of job training programs for the new replacements. Training programs, of course, become possible only when the rules or guidelines of operation have been institutionalized. New job occupants can then quickly become familiar with their responsibilities and become involved in the daily operations of the organization. The process of change has run its course, and the organization has achieved a new state of equilibrium. This equilibrium will probably remain until the recognition of the need for another new program develops—the evaluation stage —thus starting the cycle again.

A Case History of the Process of Change

As stated previously, there have been few studies of the actual process of organizational change.[10] Therefore, it is difficult to illustrate the consequences of different strategies in the stages of change outlined in the previous section. However, there is one study—the community hospital discussed in the previous chapter—that allows for a partial examination of this process. This illustration will help to clarify some of the dilemmas facing the organizational elite.

Evaluation Stage   Community Hospital had a clear-cut standard for measuring its success, at least in the area of medical education.[11] Each year prospective medical interns choose a hospital for their internship on the basis of a nation-wide matching system. Prospective interns list the hospital of their choice, and hospitals list their choice of interns. These are then matched by a computer. Because there are more intern positions available than there are applicants to fill them, some hospitals are unable to fill all of their vacancies. Community Hospital had been unsuccessful in obtaining more than one or two interns through this matching plan, although another hospital in the same city was able to fill all of its positions. This was a clear and constant reminder of failure to the decision makers of the hospital. They decided to attempt to alter this situation by adopting an extensive program of medical education that would hopefully attract a full complement of interns.

The program was both broad in scope and radical in its design. For example, it involved the addition of nine new occupational specialties to the social structure of the hospital. The organization decision makers decided to model their program on that of the university hospital, a type of hospital that is usually successful in obtaining interns. This illustrates how the force of competition may be a major factor in an organization adopting a new program, a point discussed in the previous chapter. As pointed out there, the innovation is likely to be one that was tried and proved successful in another organization. In this case, Community Hospital adopted the successful format of the university hospital.

Initiation Stage   The proposed program was both broad in scope and expensive. Because Community Hospital, like many nonprofit organizations, had a financial deficit, financial resources from outside the hospital had to be obtained to pay for this program. Several foundations were approached; and they agreed to support the program, but only for a limited period of time. In addition, the hospital had to agree to contribute some of its own financial resources to the program as an indication of its support. Thus, the hospital lost some autonomy by seeking outside support.

The elite of the hospital adopted two different strategies for hiring the men to fill the newly created positions. In most cases, they hired highly trained specialists from other hospitals. But for one of the new positions, they hired a man who was already on the staff of the hospital. The latter individual was more readily accepted by the staff than the newly recruited specialists; but the newly recruited specialists from outside the hospital had higher standards of quality and saw a need for many changes within the organization.

Implementation Stage   At first, the new specialists—a hematologist, an endocrinologist, a specialist in infectious diseases, a cardiologist, a neurologist, and full-time teachers in medicine, surgery, obstetrics-gynecology and pediatrics—tried the strategy of implementing new programs without securing the approval and cooperation of the physicians involved. This resulted in considerable resistance on the part of the physicians. The increased resistance almost resulted in the elite of the hospital withdrawing their support from the program. The new occupants later changed their strategy and discussed with the individuals affected each new program that was developed. But each time new programs were discussed, the physicians, especially those who had the most power before the addition of the medical education program, would curtail the proposals. This reduced resistance, but it frustrated the occupants of the new positions. For example, when an attempt was made to add a new teaching-ward service to the surgical service of the hospital, the surgeons, who were the main group affected, opposed the plan. The reason for their opposition was that under the suggested plan they would not have any control over the teaching rounds. These were to be conducted by the new personnel who were specialists themselves. The administration and the chief of the surgical service agreed to support the plan. When one surgeon threatened the hospital with a law suit, the administration became concerned. A compromise was reached and the surgeons were allowed to retain some control; but within a month, the new program was largely defunct.

The same plan was attempted on the pediatric service. A series of secret meetings was held, and the pediatricians threatened to resign en masse (there were ten of them) unless the new pediatric specialist was fired. The administration called the bluff of the pediatricians and they did not resign. But the full-time pediatric teacher felt his effectiveness had been destroyed because the power conflict had resulted in many interpersonal animosities.

What made some of these power struggles especially acute was that frequently the new specialists who were added to the hospital staff through the new medical education program attempted to increase their power vis-à-vis the other members of the hospital staff. They wanted complete control over their new programs and argued that this was necessary in order for them to make these effective. Those who already had considerable power in the organization were reluctant to yield any of that power to these new organizational members. The attempts on the part of the new medical specialists to gain greater power in the organization is one example of how the process of change tends to counteract the tendency toward centralization, especially during the implementation stage.

Another factor affecting the power struggle was the differences in training and skills between the newer and older medical groups. The occupants of the new jobs had all been trained in university hospitals and had received subspecialty training, that is, education beyond residency training. In contrast, most of the physicians in the hospital, especially the surgeons who had most of the power, had been trained in community hospitals; and few of them had specialty training, much less education beyond their residency. The different quality of education meant socialization to different values and ways of evaluating the success of existing programs in Community Hospital. What was clearly a need in the eyes of the new job occupants was not considered a need by the physicians in the hospital.

Still a third factor affecting the distribution of power was the gradual development of new patterns of communication—mainly horizontal—in the hospital. The new specialists, who worked full-time in the hospital made contacts with individuals in many different parts of the organization. This contact was necessary for them to accomplish their objectives, especially during the period of implementation. But this meant that new channels of communication were being established, channels not controlled by the surgeons. As Thompson has noted, this sort of communication tends to undermine an existing power structure.[12]

This study also illustrated how the addition of a new program can result in changes in other hospital activities. In order to make teaching more effective, the interns were assigned to cover only fifteen beds each, a practice common to university hospitals but unusual for community hospitals with internship and residency programs. Again the surgeons opposed the plan, but the administration supported it. (This represented an example of how the surgeons were in some cases losing power as a consequence of the implementation of this new program.) The interns were supposed to take care of emergencies involving other patients, but there was some confusion over what constituted an emergency. The nurses continued their old habits and called the interns whenever they felt it was necessary. In many cases, it was not a bona-fide emergency, so the interns stopped answering some calls. As a consequence on one occasion there was an inadequate response to a real emergency, and a patient nearly died. The administration was quite upset and a series of crisis meetings were held until guidelines for such situations were developed and agreed upon. When patterns of behavior are altered in one new program, there are likely to be incidents that create strain in other programs. The strain is likely to endure until new procedures and regulations are worked out and become habitual for those affected by the new program.

Another example of how an innovation resulted in the alteration of behavior of the lower participants was the addition of weekly grand rounds. In order for these to be effective, the medical residents had to learn how to present themselves to patients, including the skill of interviewing the patients. The physicians attached to each clinical service had to attend the rounds if there was to be any discussion of patients. The full-time teachers also instituted daily patient rounds, and the residents were required to do additional reading for these. The physicians had to cooperate by allowing their patients to be used for teaching purposes. In order to make the daily patient rounds effective, the physicians had to be willing to accept therapeutic suggestions such as the ordering of a diagnostic test or the prescribing of a drug. Although these are only two specific examples from this new program, they indicate how the addition of activities such as grand rounds and patient rounds frequently require the alteration in behavior of many other occupations in order for the new activity to become effective.

The elite faced a constant dilemma during the period of implementation. If they gave too much power to the new specialists, then the surgeons increased their resistance. If they did not, then programs were not likely to be successfully implemented. Nor was the participation of those affected by an innovation always a clear solution. Although participation did reduce resistance, it was at the expense of diluting many of the proposed changes.

Routinization Stage   The consolidation of the whole program gradually occurred. In this particular case history, the consolidation was made by the new occupational specialists themselves. The continual conflict over authority, rules, space, and other kinds of resources made continual attempts at change too difficult. A number of the specific plans in the original design of the medical education program were abandoned.

Most of the new medical personnel who originated the new medical education program eventually left the hospital, and others took their places. When the period of foundation support ended, the hospital assumed some of the costs of the program. By this time the hospital was recruiting a full complement of interns, the conflicts had subsided, and the period of change had ended.[13]

Other Approaches to Stages of Social Change

Other social scientists interested in the phenomenon of social change, whether in organizations or in total societies, have also proposed that the process of social change be conceptualized as a series of stages. These are shown in the table on page 113. A comparison among these various approaches is of interest because it provides the reader with some insight into the relative emphasis of these other researchers. It should be noted at the outset, however, that only Mann and Neff's work refers specifically to social change in organizations; Roger's work was based on individual acceptance of innovation; and Smelser's work reflects social change during the Industrial Revolution in England.[14] Despite these differences in interests and viewpoints, there is some degree of similarity in their descriptions of each stage.

Rogers' stages of social change reflect the adoption of innovative practices or activities by individuals. As such, Rogers' is a social-psychological approach to the problem of social change. In his awareness stage, the individual first becomes exposed to the innovation; in the interest stage, the

Stages in Progress of Organization Change	Rogers*	Smelser†	Mann and Neff‡
1. Evaluation	1. Awareness 2. Interest 3. Evaluation	1. Dissatisfaction with Sense of Opportunity 2. Symptoms of Disturbance 3. Handling Disturbances 4. Channeling Disturbances 5. Attempts to Specify	1. State of Organization before Change 2. Recognition of Need for Change
2. Initiation			3. Planning Change
3. Implementation	4. Trial	6. Implementation by Entrepreneurs	4. Taking Steps to make Change
4. Routinization	5. Adoption	7. Routinization	5. Stabilizing Change

* Everett Rogers, *Diffusion of Innovations* (New York: Free Press, 1962).
† Neil Smelser, *Social Change in the Industrial Revolution: An Application of Theory to the Lancashire Cotton Industry* (Chicago: University of Chicago Press, 1959).
‡ Floyd C. Mann and F. W. Neff, *Managing Major Change in Organizations* (Ann Arbor, Mich.: Foundation for Research on Human Behavior, 1961).

individual seeks additional information; and in the evaluation stage, the individual "mentally applies the innovation to his present and anticipated future situation." [15] We have grouped all these activities into the single stage of evaluation. Because Rogers' approach involves a decision to innovate by a single individual and our concern with organizations means that we are concerned with a collective decision to innovate, there are obviously differences between us, but a parallel remains; namely, this stage involves the seeking of information and exploration of the possible consequences of innovation.

Rogers has no stage similar to our stage of initiation during which organizations must obtain money and men in order to implement the innovation. Such concerns are less crucial aspects of individual acceptance of innovation. During Rogers' trial stage, the individual tries the innovation in a limited fashion to determine its feasibility for complete adoption. This is analogous to our implementation stage. Finally, in Rogers' adoption stage, the individual decides to utilize the innovation fully, which is similar to our routinization stage. Obviously, there are some differences in the content of Rogers' stages and our own owing to the differences in the type of unit that is adopting an innovation: individuals versus organizations. But, there does seem to be some overlap in the two processes of innovation.

Smelser's work refers to the process of structural differentiation in the cotton industry in Britain between 1770 and 1840. Smelser is also using a unit of analysis that is different from our own; namely, a total society and its economic development. Factory organizations were certainly the units through which this differentiation became manifested, but Smelser is little concerned with the impact of new technology on the social structure of the factory itself. There is only a loose correspondence between his first four stages and our evaluation stage. A common element between the two, however, is the recognition of the need and possibility of change. Smelser's fifth stage, attempts to specify, is analogous to our initiation stage in that both refer to the obtaining of adequate resources in order to implement the social change. Smelser seems to be referring to the availability of technological developments in the cotton industry. During this stage in our model there is the problem of obtaining adequately trained personnel as well as adequate financial resources to make the change. Smelser's sixth stage, implementation by entrepreneurs, is certainly analogous to our own implementation stage. During this stage the innovation is brought into reality. For both Smelser and ourselves, the last step is routinization, a stage in which an attempt is made to regain equilibrium. It seems clear that the differences in the phenomenon that Smelser was describing and our own are greater than the similarities. He was discussing the process of structural differentiation of a society, but we have discussed a much more limited phenomenon. Still, this comparison of the process of social change is fruitful because it helps to amplify our previous discussion.

Only Mann and Neff's description of the stages of social change refer to organizations per se. Their first two stages, the state of the organization before change and the recognition of a need for change, clearly overlap with our evaluation stage. Their stage of planning the change combines some elements from both our evaluation and our initiation stage. By planning the change, they are referring to the clarification and definition of objectives, the development and review of alternative courses of action, and determination of proper strategy and tactics. These are activities that we have included in the evaluation stage. But Mann and Neff also include in this stage identifying and developing needed skills, which we have classified in the implementation stage. They also include descriptions of effective power equalization techniques at this stage, which we have discussed as one of the dilemmas of implementation. Mann and Neff's final stage, stabilizing change, is similar to our routinization stage, however. One of the difficulties in making exact comparisons between Mann and Neff's description of stages in social change and our own is that their discussion is much more oriented to the practitioner's point of view. Their work is designed to alert change agents to problems of human relations; thus there is not exact comparability between their approach and our own.

Although there are clearly differences in approaches, units of analysis, and emphases, we have underlined the similarities of these approaches to our own in describing stages of social change. The contrasts between these different approaches raise other problems about the process of change. The question could logically be raised: Why have you chosen to discuss four stages? Smelser had seven; Rogers and Mann and Neff had five. Although the selection of four stages is rather arbitrary, these stages do focus attention on some of the major problems that emerge in the process of social change in complex organizations.

Conclusions

Again we have tried to make our understanding of organizations in general and social change in particular more complete by examining the process of change itself. This makes clear the persistent tug of war between the need to solve a problem that originates in the environment and the need to adopt a solution that is viable for the organization. This is the dilemma between maximizing change and minimizing conflicts that continually confronts organizational leaders.

5 Limitations, Predictions, and Problems

Throughout, our purpose has been to explain change from two vantage points: external and internal factors. This explanation will permit us to make some predictions about organizational evolution as well as draw implications for organizational policy. But before such issues as these are discussed, it is necessary to consider some of the limitations of our discussions. There are two types of qualifications that we shall make: First, the consideration that other variables may account for organizational change; second, the possibility that there are other approaches that one may employ in understanding this phenomenon. Our eight characteristics by no means represent an exhaustive list of organizational characteristics. A consideration of other variables may provide the reader an opportunity to qualify our remarks and realize the exceptions to our basic ideas. Our approach is by no means the only one that is utilized in the study of organizations. In fact, there are several alternative approaches that have been used. Although these other approaches do not seem to be the most appropriate way to study the phenomenon of organizational change, the reader should become aware of them so that he can better evaluate our approach. These limitations will be discussed in the first section of this chapter.

One of the main reasons suggested in Chapter 1 for studying change in organizations was to acquire an appreciation of how they have evolved over time. The past and the future of organizational life can be approximated from an understanding of its present form. With the environmental factors discussed in Chapter 3 some reasons for the variations in the nature of organizations at different historical points can be suggested. In particular, we are interested in suggesting the form organizational life is likely to take in the future. If we can make some estimate of such characteristics ten, twenty, or even thirty years from now, then we can anticipate some of the problems that future generations may have to face. We can possibly even begin to work toward avoiding them altogether. Another important reason suggested in Chapter 1 for the importance of the study of organizational change was that it could provide the possibility of some measure of control over the direction of this evolution. These hypotheses point out the future implications of certain types of arrangements. Decision makers can make conscious choices that will lead toward static or dynamic organizational forms. Organizational policy can then be articulated with the values of these decision makers and the members of society; that is, values regarding the relative importance of efficiency versus quality, or new programs versus morale, can be expressed in policies and programs of organizations. Policy need not be completely subjected to the vagaries of the situation, but instead it can be a conscious articulation of fundamental human beliefs with organizational decision making. Ramifications such as these are discussed in the third section of this chapter.

Limitations and Qualifications

There are two ways in which our present analysis of organizational change has been of restricted scope. First, we chose to limit our discussion to a sociological perspective, and in the process we neglected psychological variables that may play a part in organizational change. Second, we chose to limit our approach to the study of what we consider to be key organizational characteristics; that is, we have neglected several other sociological approaches and, hence, other sociological variables. For example, we chose to limit our analysis to a consideration of only eight organizational characteristics, including program change. By specifying some of these other perspectives and approaches, we are pointing out the limitations of our present analysis. This discussion will also provide some suggestion for future areas of theoretical development and empirical research.

It is a truism that social life is complex, but it is not always understood that the pathway to understanding that complexity is the road of simplification. As we suggested in Chapter 1, it is better to study the interrelationships between a few variables, admitting that they hardly capture all of reality, before attempting to complicate the analysis. Once a few relationships are mastered, additional variables may then be added. Gradually more and more facts may then be explained, permitting the explanation of increasingly complex events.

Although there is more than one sociological approach to the study of organizations, and certainly many other organizational characteristics that we have not included here, we feel that our approach and the list of characteristics is the best one for understanding organizational change. This, of course, does not mean that we are correct. We shall specify our reasons for eliminating certain variables and let the reader judge for himself the accuracy of our claim.

Psychological Perspectives Although we feel that there is no inherent reason to exclude a psychological perspective in our discussion of organizational change, there are certain issues involving the elimination of a psychological perspective that need to be at least discussed, even though it is not possible to resolve them. The major issue is that some have claimed that it is possible to reduce all sociological variables to psychological ones. According to this line of reasoning, often called *psychological reductionism*, an organization is highly centralized because its key decision makers have authoritarian personalities; similarly, one may argue that an organization is highly formalized because it is full of persons having rigid or bureaucratic personalities.

A related perspective argues that not all sociological propositions are psychological, but that no general sociological propositions have been developed.[1] Thus, while not arguing psychological reductionism as such, this position maintains that there is currently mislabeling of what sociologists feel are propositions about collectivities. It is impossible to settle this issue, however, until much more is known about the relationship between organizational structure and individual personality; but some evidence relevant to this issue can be examined.

Selznick has suggested that organizations recruit specific personalities at particular points in time to meet organizational needs.[2] During times of instability, for example, organizations may recruit persons who can tolerate ambiguity, uncertainty, and change. Similarly, during a period of stabilization organizations may attempt to hire persons who are desirous of order and stability in their immediate world. In a study of social change in several organizations, Mann and Hoffman have suggested that if an organization is experiencing a high degree of change, there will be a turnover in personnel, with those personalities desiring greater stability leaving the organization.[3]

These two processes—organizational recruitment and individual self-selection—could lead to the same result: the creation of a climate of common values and attitudes among staff members about the desirability and appropriateness of social change.

In our own research on social change in social welfare and health organizations, we made an attempt to gather information that would reflect on this issue.[4] We asked the members of each organization a series of questions designed to elicit their attitudes towards change in general. For example, we asked whether or not the respondent agreed that there was a need for change right now, whether or not the respondent agreed that there was a perennial need for change, and whether or not the respondent liked change.

These attitudinal measures were developed by Sister Maria Augusta Neal in a study of the Catholic clergy.[5] She had noted that some people appear to be motivated primarily by self-interest, but others seem to be motivated by higher values and ideals. Combining these two basic motivational orientations with either prochange or antichange attitudes provided Sister Neal with four personality types: the "prophet," who is prochange and motivated by higher ideals; the "organization man," who is prochange but motivated by self-interest; the "priest," who is antichange and motivated by higher ideals; and the "local organization man," who is antichange and motivated by self-interest. The religious labels reflect the nature of her sample, that is, priests in a Catholic diocese.

What is especially interesting about her work is that she found that each of these basic types of orientation was related to certain kinds of defense mechanisms, suggesting that she had indeed tapped basic personality dimensions. Those individuals who were value oriented and prochange were less likely to use any defense mechanisms and when they did, to blame themselves, that is, they blamed themselves for the lack of collective change. At the other extreme, individuals motivated by self-interest and antichange were most likely to use defense mechanisms, in particular, rationalization and denial of the existence of problems. In addition, she found that the four types of personality had a variety of different attitude responses about specific problems of the church and racial equality.

Sister Neal's measures of attitudes toward change are neither exhaustive, nor necessarily the most accurate, but they do provide some opportunity to examine empirically the question of personality and social structure as they relate to social change. We used her four scales in our own study, but when we factor analyzed responses to these items, we discovered that the two extremes in her study—the value and prochange type and the self-interest and antichange type—formed two factors, eliminating the other two types. In other words, those in favor of change were motivated by a sense of values, and those opposed to change were motivated by a sense of self-interest. We related these two scales to the relative rates of program change in our sixteen health and welfare organizations. In particular, we were interested in knowing what effect the job occupants with different attitudes about the desirability of change would have on the rate of program change during the three years following the measurement of these attitudes. The values and prochange factor was positively related to the number of new programs ($r = .22$), but the self-interests and antichange factor was also positively related to number of new programs ($r = .13$). These results were, therefore, somewhat contradictory and inconclusive. The number of occupational specialties in 1964, an indicator of complexity, had the strongest relationship with program change ($r = .64$); but the degree of professional activism of the staffs of these agencies, another measure of complexity, was also highly related ($r = .42$). The aspect of complexity, the degree of professional training, was practically unrelated to the amount of program change ($r = .09$). The degree of participation in organizational decision making, one of our measures of centralization, was also more strongly related to program change than were attitudes of individual members. The results of our study clearly suggest that structural properties were much more highly associated with the rate of program change than attitudes toward change.[6]

This implies that the structure of an organization may be more crucial for the successful implementation of change than the particular blend of personality types in an organization.

Although this small piece of evidence by no means resolves the question of whether sociological variables are better predictors of social change than psychological attitudes it certainly supports our choice of approaches. But there are also logical reasons why we have focused on a sociological rather than a psychological perspective in the study of organizational change. We believe that collective properties are best explained by other collective properties, such as our organizational characteristics. In most of the sciences, explanation occurs on the same level of abstraction; thus physical properties are explained by other physical properties, chemical properties by other chemical properties, biological properties by other biological properties. Similarly we feel that sociological variables, that is, properties of collectives such as an organization, should ultimately be explained by other sociological properties and not psychological ones. This is not to say that there can not be covariation on each level of analysis; this is entirely possible. In fact, there are probably psychological analogs for each of the structural properties that we have outlined. For example, although we conceive of the stratification system of an organization as a collective property, it is entirely possible that the differential rewards implicit in a highly stratified organization may result in the maximization of certain types of defense mechanisms and affect the self-evaluations of organizational members. And similarly, in a highly egalitarian organization there may be a high utilization of certain other types of defense mechanisms by organizational members. This would be an example of how social structure affects personality.[7] It is entirely conceivable that the personalities in an organization may modify certain aspects of organizational structure. This would be an example of personality affecting social structure. We are admitting that there may be important relations between these levels of abstraction, that is, that psychological properties may affect sociological properties and vice-versa.

On the other hand, we argue that the amount of explanatory power of these approaches is likely to be far less than the explanatory power of variables on the same level of abstraction, that is, the interrelationships between two structural properties such as complexity and program change or the interrelationships between two psychological properties such as the need for achievement and certain types of psychological defenses.

Still another important approach to organizations is that of leadership.[8] For example, some organizations may be more dynamic than others because they have charismatic leaders, men who are imbued with certain personality attributes that permit them to mobilize, affect, and channel it into support for higher rates of organizational change. Eliot of Harvard may have been such a man. It is difficult to say that this was the case in DuPont or in the case of the prison reported in Chapter 3. Admittedly the personalities of individuals vary as we have already suggested in Chapter 3, and the use of persuasion is an important factor in reducing resistance to social change. Similarly, the charismatic leader may have other qualities that are essential to effect change. Unfortunately, there has been inadequate research on the relative importance of leadership style as opposed to structural properties in understanding change dynamics. It may well be that everything we have said in this book about structural change is simply a function of variations in leadership style—the charismatic leader in the highly changing organization and the traditional or "caretaker" leader in nonchanging organizations. Thus, this factor of leadership style should be considered as a possible qualification of our present discussion. We will have to leave this an open question until social research is able to evaluate systematically the importance of leadership as opposed to social structure for organizational change.

Other Sociological Approaches   There are several other sociological approaches to the study of organization in general and organizational change in particular. These are (1) the study of organizational goals, (2) the study of organizational technology, and (3) the study of human relations in organizations.

ORGANIZATIONAL GOALS Some sociologists believe that the best focal point in understanding organizations is the examination of organizational goals, that is, the examination not only of the formal statements about the organization's objectives, but also of what the organization actually seems to be accomplishing, what sociologists call operative goals. These sociologists argue that by knowing both the formal and operative goals, one can understand the functioning of the organization.[9] For example, they contrast mental hospitals or correctional institutions having treatment goals with those having custodial goals. In some cases there are comparisons of organizations with totally different types of formal goals, such as hospitals with a goal of patient care and economic organizations with the goal of profit.

One difficulty with the goal approach is that it tells us little about organizational evolution. Although it is certainly true that the alteration of goals may mean the alteration of other internal processes, the goal approach tells us little about the future of the organization.[10] Nor does this approach have much to say about the changing characteristics of organizations even when the goals remain the same. Perhaps the major weakness of the goal approach is that it focuses on the content and not the form of organizational life. As Cassirer has suggested, modern science has learned that the approach that allows for the development of hypotheses is an emphasis on the formal properties of the unit of analysis and not an emphasis on the substance or content of that unit.[11]

At the same time, an organization with a goal of research is probably more likely to have a higher rate of change than an organization without this goal. But if this is true, it is not so much a consequence of this goal, but rather a consequence of having the characteristics that maximize social change, that is, organizational characteristics associated with the dynamic style of organizational life.

One of the problems in the study of organizational goals is their measurement. The charter may make one statement about goals, and the decision makers may have an entirely different objective in mind. The public statements about goals may not correspond with the actual state of affairs existing in the organization. The officials of one university may state that the objective is to teach, and yet faculty members are promoted on the basis of research publications. The doctors of a hospital may state that they are concerned with the quality of patient care, and yet decisions made in the hospital may reflect only a concern with an increase in private income. Managers of a manufacturing plant may state that their concern is the continued employment of the workers, and yet corporate decisions may reflect a continued desire for hiring fewer and fewer workers by automating. Which are the goals of the organization—public statements or private utterances, official documents or day-to-day decisions? Understandably, the student of organizational life who takes this approach must try to understand both formal and operative goals. But how does he study operative goals? It is often necessary to spend a great deal of time in the organization trying to understand the internal operation of organizational life.[12] Eventually, the researcher comes to have some understanding of the organization, and he conceptualizes his understanding in terms of the goals of the organization. For example, in a study of a hospital, the researchers conceptualized the organization as changing from custodial to therapeutic goals.[13] Studies such as these are interesting. There is the continual problem of adequate specification of the nature of the major variable, organizational goals, as well as its measurement. This becomes particularly acute in measuring organizational goals in a comparative framework in which many different kinds of organizations are involved. However, the structural approach seems more appropriate because it specifies many dimensions of organizational life that may be implicit within the highly diffuse idea of organizational goals.

ORGANIZATIONAL TECHNOLOGY Another approach, analogous to the study of goals, is the examination of the technology of a particular organization. It is similar because it takes one major variable, technology, and attempts to show how many aspects of organization life are a function of a particular type of technology.

Blauner attempted to relate four major kinds of technology to worker satisfaction.[14] The four industries he describes are printing, textiles, automobile manufacture, and chemical processing. The printing industry is organized in essentially a craft organization. Job satisfaction is quite high because workers are more likely to have control over the pace of work, the process of work, and the product of work. The characteristics of this type of technology were most similar to work arrangements prior to the Industrial Revolution. The technology of the textile industry allows less freedom in work and less job autonomy than that of the printing industry; and, consequently, job satisfaction is lower among workers in the textile industry than among those in printing. The mass production technology of the assembly line allows even less control over the pace of work, over the process of work, and over the final product; consequently, workers in the automobile industry are even more dissatisfied or alienated. On the other hand, the continuous process arrangements of the highly automated chemical industry permits workers greater control over their work. Blauner extrapolates the future implications of his findings to suggest that not mass production technologies, but industries with highly automated technologies such as chemical processing are likely to be most characteristic of the future. The implication is not a decrease in job satisfaction in the future, but perhaps a trend toward higher job satisfaction as automated industries become more prevalent. This brief description of Blauner's rather provocative book is an example of how technology can be related to other organizational characteristics. Blauner did not directly discuss the problem of organizational change, however. Stanley Udy has also suggested that technology in nonindustrial societies is related to the development of particular kinds of bureaucratic organization.[15]

Perhaps the most important study from this perspective, and indeed one of the most provocative books about organizational behavior that has been written in recent years, is Joan Woodward's *Industrial Organization: Theory and Practice*.[16] Woodward studied one hundred industrial firms in Great Britain and showed how variations in technology were related to variations in organizational structure. She defined three major categories of technology: (1) unit and small batch production in which plants made prototypes, fabricated large equipment in stages and produced custom tailored units; (2) large batch and mass production in which goods were produced in large quantities such as on an assembly line; and (3) process production such as intermittent production of chemicals in multipurpose plants or continuous-flow production of such things as gases and liquids.

She found that there were more levels of management in the organizations with complex technologies, that is, group 3 above, and the fewest levels of management in organizations with the simplest technologies, that is, group 1 above. As a corollary she found that firms with complex technologies had a lower ratio of managers to supervisors than the firms with simple technologies; that is, a manager in process firms with more complex technology supervised less people than those in firms with simpler and more routine technologies. In the process firms graduate trainees were dispersed through the line and staff; this was less true of organizations with the more routine technologies.

Such findings suggest the utility of this particular approach to the study of organizational behavior. One of the chief characteristics of such an approach is that a single variable, technology, is used as the focal concept to understand variations in organizational structure and dynamics.[17] Although technology does have some effect on social organization, there appear to be few hypotheses relating technology to the problem of organizational change. The applicability of the concept of technology to nonindustrial organizations is less obvious. That is, it is more difficult to characterize the "mechanisms or processes by which an organization turns out its products or services" in "people-changing" organizations such as health, social welfare, and educational organizations.[18] One way would be to try to characterize the degree of routineness of work procedures, although at present there are some difficulties in both the conceptualization and measurement of this aspect of technology. All we can say is that in some ways the kind of technology affects organizational structure, and this in turn may influence the degree of social change in an organization. For example in Blauner's study, the craft and automated technologies of the printing and chemical industries, respectively, appeared to be associated with a relatively decentralized, nonformalized structural arrangement. In contrast, the textile and automobile industries appeared to be much more centralized and formalized. Until there is more research in this area, all we can do is to indicate that technology undoubtedly affects organizational structure and thus the rate of change. Too little information is available about this approach to make any statement beyond these brief and limited speculations.

HUMAN RELATIONS   We have already commented on this approach to organizational analysis in the previous chapter. Essentially the human relations approach stresses how members of an organization feel about their leaders and the organization in general. As such, it is primarily a social psychological approach; but since it does emphasize certain dynamics that we have discussed under the rubric of centralization, it seems appropriate to discuss it as an alternative sociological approach to organizations. There are numerous studies and books that have been written from this approach.[19] In a recent review and summary of this approach, Harold J. Leavitt points out that a common assumption of this approach is that one changes the world by changing the people within it.[20] In our terms, this means that one changes organization by changing organizational members. One of the fundamental ways to change people is to give them more power, with the assumption that most people desire to have greater participation in decisions in the organizations that shape their lives. Thus, if people participate more—what Leavitt calls "power equalization"—then they are more likely to accede to demands for social change. This "power equalization" approach additionally emphasizes morale; it is assumed that power equalization leads to greater morale, which in turn makes the implementation of social change easier.

We really have no quarrel with this approach. In fact, it is implicit in our earlier discussion of the relationship between both centralization and program change as well as morale and social change. Our preference is to discuss these phenomena in the context of organizational properties, however. The power equalization approach really emphasizes the how-to-do-it aspect of organizational change. That is certainly a legitimate area of inquiry, but beyond the scope of this book. On the other hand, this approach can give the reader who is interested in the actual process of how individuals react and accept social change a good understanding of such dynamics. In other words, the power equalization approach is not at all inconsistent with some of the major ideas of this book. The differences between our approach and this one are twofold: other factors may be equally, or perhaps more, important to the understanding of organizational change than the degree of centralization and morale of the organization; and the conceptualization of this power equalization phenomenon in terms of structural properties rather than individual properties seems more appropriate.

Other Sociological Variables   Not only are there other sociological approaches to the study of organizational behavior, but there are some additional sociological variables that are entirely consistent with this structural approach which we have not discussed. Two of these are the size of the organization and the financial arrangements under which the organization must operate.

Pugh and his colleagues recently reviewed a large number

of sociological studies of organization.[21] On the basis of their review they developed four classifications of organizational variables: performance variables, structural variables, contextual variables, and activity. The first two kinds of variables, namely, performance and structural, are similar in many ways to the kinds of variables that are used in this analysis. Their performance variables of production, productivity, and morale, are similar to our concepts of production, efficiency, and job satisfaction. Their variable of specialization is similar to our variable of complexity; both of us use centralization in a similar manner. They distinguish between formalization and standardization with relative emphasis on the use of written records; whereas, we choose to combine these two ideas under the single concept of formalization. The discussion of contextual variables by Pugh and his colleagues includes several variables that were not used in Chapter 3. Perhaps the most common sociological variable that is not included in the analysis here is the size of the organization, that is, the total number of organizational members, excluding customers or clients. Size is an ubiquitous variable in the sociological literature, but it has been used in several different ways.[22] Reviews of studies relating size to aspects both of centralization and formalization are largely inconsistent, however, at least on the basis of research that has been accomplished to date.[23]

There are several reasons why size may have different consequences for a factor such as complexity, and, thus, ultimately for the rate of organizational change. If the hiring of additional persons means the addition of new occupational specialties, then increasing size probably leads to a higher rate of organizational change for reasons argued previously. If the hiring of additional men means only the addition of more job occupants in existing occupations, and no new occupational specialties, then increasing size may result in increasing centralization and lack of organizational change. It is because increasing size means different things in different contexts that we have eliminated it from consideration.

Another variable is the amount of finances available to an

organization. New programs or new techniques require funds. Organizations, whether profit making or nonprofit making, may very well institute more changes if they have ample funds. At the same time, increased financial resources can be allocated to expand production, that is, the number of clients served or the number of products manufactured, rather than to increase the number of new programs, services, or products. In our interviews in welfare agencies, mental hospitals, and schools, the directors were asked what they would do with increased funds if they were available. The replies to this question were quite variegated. Some directors indicated their concern with expansion in the number of clients served and reduction of the case load of organizational members, because in some cases the workload exceeded acceptable limits. Other directors were more concerned with the addition of new programs and services, with no anticipated increase in clients served. In other words, increased funds can be employed differently to emphasize either an increase in the quantity of clients served or the quality of clients' services.[24] The amount of finances, like the size of the organization, can have two opposite consequences for organizational change. On the other hand, lack of adequate financial resources may restrict the possibility of program change in spite of the orientation and commitments of the membership.

Some other more obvious organizational variables that could be considered are those relating to organizational communications, conflict, and mechanisms of social control. In many cases, however, our discussion has included references to these aspects of organizational life. Our approach does not lend itself to the inclusion of these variables as structural properties, however.

Predictions

It is impossible to determine the origin of the first organizations. Udy's study of organizations in nonindustrial societies suggests that even in the simplest of societies, organizations proved useful and were utilized to achieve man's need for food.[25] Although we can speculate little about the origin of organizations, we can say some things about their development, particularly in the last few thousand years. This long view of organizations provides some insight into the future of organizational life. It is always hazardous to project past trends into the future, especially when these trends have occurred over several millennia, but it would appear to be a safer procedure than just projecting a trend based on an interval of a few decades.

Organizational Past   When man became able to cultivate fields, and especially when he became capable of storing food surpluses, the conditions were established for the proliferation of large-scale organizations, not only in agriculture and mining, but in government, military, manufacturing, and other spheres of society. By the time of the Roman Empire, organization was an essential part of mankind's existence.

During the Roman Empire, a highly centralized, formalized, and stratified structure that provided high volume of production at relatively low costs predominated. Most of the workers were slaves. The differences in rewards between the slaves and managers were enormous. The slaves did a few simple operations that were repeated endlessly. This formalization of tasks allowed for the easy replacement of workers if one died.

A study of nonindustrial societies, including the Roman Empire, indicates that most agricultural societies had centralized governments and centralized economic units.[26] In societies in which there was no written language, as, for example, the Inca Empire, organizations were more likely to have characteristics of the static style. Although there were some organizations that had characteristics of the dynamic style, especially those in arts and crafts, these were by no means the more typical or dominant form of organization.

As the centuries passed, a number of changes occurred, especially in Western societies. There was a slow, but steady, accumulation of knowledge. It became more and more essential to train people as the tasks became more complicated, that is, as technology became more sophisticated. The accumulation of knowledge was reflected in the creation of new occupations.

The proliferation of occupations and the lengthening of training has resulted in a steady increase in the complexity of organizations, as well as the creation of new organizations as new products and services have been developed. As a consequence, the long-term historical trend has been the movement from the static to the dynamic style of organizational life. Governments, even in autocratic countries, have become more decentralized in their decision making, and more and more specialists and others lower in the hierarchy of government are allowed to make recommendations. Although the separation of tasks into a few simple operations was necessary when machines were crude and labor was unskilled, this procedure becomes less essential as technology gains in sophistication and labor gains in education. The important point is that growth in the complexity of organizations appears to be accelerating, especially in industrialized societies, and this acceleration leads to speculations about what the future organizational forms are likely to be.

Organizational Future　It is hard to imagine how future historians will assess the world changes since the end of World War II, but a number of significant developments can be listed. One of the most significant changes is the steadily increasing percent of the Gross National Product (GNP) of the United States that has been allocated to the acquiring of more knowledge. The percentage of the GNP allocated to basic research has grown by a steady 16 percent since 1953, although the amount allocated to applied research has only been growing at the rate of 11 percent since then.[27] Although much of this money is spent by the federal government, more and more private enterprises are allocating funds to research as a mechanism for organizational survival. A dramatic example of this is found in the drug industry. Drug companies spent five percent of all sales in 1947 for research and development; but by

1959, this had grown to over eight percent. Although this trend will not necessarily increase linearly, it is difficult to estimate the consequences of this pursuit of knowledge, because no other society in history has allocated such a large share of its human and material resources to the development of knowledge.

Simultaneously, the United States has placed a much greater emphasis on the importance of education. There are a variety of reasons for this action. The proportion of high school graduates going to college, both male and female, has more than doubled since the end of World War II. The number of graduate degrees is increasing at an even faster rate.[28] The present projections for the labor force indicate the following changes between 1940 and 1970. In 1940 there were twice as many unskilled workers as there were professionals and twice as many skilled workers as there were managers or proprietors. It is estimated that in 1970 there will be more professionals than unskilled laborers and almost as many managers and proprietors as skilled laborers. In other words, perhaps as much as 50 percent of the labor force will be in white collar occupations, that is, sales, clerical, managerial, or professional occupations.

Although there is a natural limit to the number of years that can be spent acquiring an education, there are two new developments that suggest that a college education in the 1970s may be more meaningful than it presently is. First, the standards of excellence are being increased perhaps as a consequence of student complaints about mass education. Students want more individual attention. Second, the educational emphasis is shifting from knowledge of facts to theoretical knowledge. Thinking, instead of memory, is becoming more important as it can allow for much greater flexibility in later life. Insofar as the various disciplines become more theoretical, the human mind becomes able to store vast quantities of knowledge summarized in a few formulas and the pace of learning can be accelerated. Nor is the enrichment of college and graduate programs the only new trend in our society. More and more business firms, government agencies, hospitals, and other kinds of organizations are relying upon refresher courses and summer institutes as a means of keeping their personnel abreast of the explosion in knowledge created by this intensified research activity.

The increased wealth of the society, itself partially a consequence of the expansion of knowledge, allows the decision makers of organizations to invest heavily in the machinery created by the advances in knowledge. As more and more manufacturers automate, they reduce their need for formalization and unskilled labor and instead increase their need for complexity and skilled labor. The nation only needs a certain amount of food, clothing, and shelter. As the manufacturers have satisfied these demands, the population becomes more and more interested in, and demanding of services. This demand is reflected in the labor force of which over one-half are now employed in providing services. Simultaneously, the organizations that offer services are becoming a more dominant factor in the society. The nation's schools, hospitals, and welfare agencies are employing more and more people and accounting for a larger share of the total wealth of the society. Both product and service organizations will be placing more and more emphasis on the quality of their output as opposed to the quantity.

As new products and services are invented, organizations will be competing with a larger and larger number of organizations and finding themselves dependent upon an ever-increasing number of organizations. Nor will this competition be limited to the United States. Increasingly the societies that have gone through industrialization will become more and more interdependent as it becomes increasingly more difficult for any one society, regardless of its wealth, to provide for the many tastes and desires of its citizens.

In summary, organizations in societies such as the United States appear to be evolving toward the dynamic form. This evolution is a consequence of both expanding knowledge, which necessitates the existence of complex organizations, and of expanding wealth, which provides the resources that permit organizations to be complex. But what are the problems that flow from this evolution, if any? Can we make any recommendations that would ease the impact of this evolution? These issues are discussed in the next and final section of this book.

Problems and Recommendations

The great advantage of hypotheses is that they allow us to anticipate at least some of the problems and to suggest at least some recommendations for ameliorating these problems. The hypotheses of Chapter 2 suggest that if the elite of the organization decide to place an emphasis on the quality of their product or service or if they have a conscious policy of creating a high rate of program change, the best organizational structure to facilitate such policies is high complexity, low centralization, low formalization, and low stratification—the dynamic style of organizational life. In contrast, those of the elite who prefer a policy of high volume of production and high efficiency are advised to maintain the opposite organizational characteristics—the static style. We are not arguing that any one style is necessarily best, but instead that particular structures are best adapted to particular kinds of problems and desired solutions.

In the previous section, we have suggested that the environment in the United States is changing rapidly. There are strong pressures that push organizations increasingly toward the dynamic style. The increased emphasis on research and development means higher rates of program change. Organizations will probably have to establish research and development departments, as did U.S. Steel and other members of the steel industry, in order to survive. Changes in the labor market mean a greater availability of highly trained occupational specialists. Organizations that hire the new specialists may have a competitive edge. As soon as one organization hires a sales forecaster, its competitors are likely to do so too. Nor is this competition limited to profit-making organizations. Universities, hospitals, and schools compete with one another as well. Thus, organizations will probably be forced to increase their rates of program change as well as their degree of complexity. If they do, they will eventually change other organizational characteristics as well, such as centralization, formalization, and stratification. As was suggested in Chapter 3, these variables form parts of a social system, and, therefore, if one is altered, the others will be changed as well. Decision makers may speed up this process by making deliberate decisions about change. This speed may become particularly important in order to solve problems of coordination, as the case of Du Pont illustrates. The organization that is increasing its complexity is advised to reduce centralization, formalization, and stratification.

This discussion involves a basic problem known as cultural lag. This concept, as espoused by Ogburn, postulated that there is a lag in the development of appropriate forms of social organization to meet the problems created by advancing technology.[29] The dynamic form of organization is more suited to closing this gap than other organizational forms because the characteristics of this form of organization help to facilitate the process not only of introducing innovations, but also of making appropriate adaptations to them. For the organization that for whatever reasons must adopt new techniques continuously, the dynamic style is the most appropriate form of social organization.

In the process of adopting new programs, especially when there is a shift in the rate of program change, the organization faces a series of dilemmas. Although an organization with a dynamic style can facilitate the initiation and implementation of programs, this does not reduce or eliminate all resistance to them. There are always some vested interests affected by the addition of new programs. In Chapter 4, we have discussed the magnitude of some of these dilemmas. Although we can not provide solutions to all these problems, the discussion at least makes some of the choices faced by the organizational elite more apparent. In general, change creates conflict and the organizational elite who are interested in making innovations must be willing to pay this price.

There is another price that must be paid in the dynamic style of organizational life: the price of lower efficiency, that is, lower costs per unit of production. High rates of change and an emphasis on quality as opposed to quantity are costly. Not all organizations can afford to pay the price. Again, this is a question of values, which may vary, depending on the particular organizational circumstances. We have tried in this book to make some of these value choices clearer so that the organizational elite can make their decisions more intelligently. A theory of organizational change should not only attempt to explain what needs to be done in order to implement innovation, but also to outline the costs involved and to specify some probable effects of change as well. And this is what we have tried to do.

Notes

1 The Anatomy of Organizations

1. See Herbert Blumer, "Collective Behavior," in A. M. Lee (ed.), *New Outline of the Principles of Sociology* (New York: Barnes and Noble, 1946), pp. 165–222; Richard T. LaPiere, *Collective Behavior* (New York: McGraw-Hill, 1938); Neil J. Smelser, *Theory of Collective Behavior* (New York: Free Press, 1963); Ralph H. Turner and Lewis M. Killian, *Collective Behavior* (Englewood Cliffs, N. J.: Prentice-Hall, 1957).

2. See Peter Blau and W. Richard Scott, *Formal Organizations: A Comparative Approach* (San Francisco: Chandler, 1962); Theodore Caplow, *Principles of Organization* (New York: Harcourt, Brace, and World, 1964); and Amitai Etzioni (ed.), *Complex Organizations: A Sociological Reader* (New York: Holt, Rinehart, and Winston, 1961) for general discussions about the name for organizations and their characteristics and problems.

3. Even one of the first tasks of man, finding food, was organized. See Stanley Udy, Jr., *Organization of Work: A Comparative Analysis of Production among Nonindustrial Peoples* (New Haven, Conn.: Human Relations Area File Press, 1959).

4. For an excellent discussion of man's adaptability, see Theodosius Dobzhansky, *Mankind Evolving: The Evolution of the Human Species* (New Haven, Conn.: Yale University Press, 1962). For a broader point of view, see Pierre Teilhard de Chardin, *The Phenomenon of Man,* Bernard Wall (tr.), (New York: Harper & Row, 1959).

5. For the general logic behind this procedure which is a relatively new one in the social sciences, and especially in the field of sociology, see Ernst Cassirer, *Substance and Function and Einstein's Theory of Relativity,* W. C. Swabey and Marie C. Swabey (tr.) (New York: Dover, 1953), Chapter 1.

6. Talcott Parsons, "Sociological Approach to Organizations," *Administrative Science Quarterly,* 1 (June 1956), 63–85.

7. Not all organizational sociologists agree with such a distinction. Caplow, *op. cit.*, Chapter 1, would prefer to use the family as an example of an organization.

8. See Caplow, *ibid.*, for several amusing examples. For several concrete examples providing illustrations of the several basic kinds of organization, see Joan Woodward, *Industrial Organization: Theory and Practice* (London: Oxford University Press, 1965), especially Chapter 7.

9. Theodore Caplow, *The Sociology of Work* (Minneapolis: University of Minnesota Press, 1954) has a discussion of some of the more famous family businesses. For a discussion of the change from family-oriented businesses to the development of industrial enterprises, see Neil Smelser, *Social Change in the Industrial Revolution: An Application of Theory to the Lancashire Cotton Industry* (Chicago: University of Chicago Press, 1959).

10. Each of these terms is used to describe a construct involving many characteristics. For a good discussion of some of these terms with a concrete research example, see Robert Redfield, *The Folk Culture of Yucatan* (Chicago: University of Chicago Press, 1949). The idea of primary groups is from Charles Horton Cooley, *Social Organization: A Study of the Larger Mind* (New York: Scribner, 1909). We are following Parsons' emphasis on the idea of specificity, but there are other elements involved in these ideas. See Talcott Parsons, *The Social System* (Glencoe, Ill.: Free Press, 1951), Chapter 3. Also see Blau and Scott, *op. cit.*, Chapter 1.

11. Robert Blauner, *Alienation and Freedom: The Factory Worker and His Industry* (Chicago: University of Chicago Press, 1964), pp. 24–26.

12. Blau and Scott, *op. cit.*, pp. 45–49. Their other three categories of formal organizations—business concerns, service organizations, and commonweal organizations—are more consistent with our definition of organizations.

13. Compare Amos H. Hawley, *Human Ecology* (New York: The Ronald Press, 1950), p. 180.

14. For a discussion of how this approach affects the way that data can be summarized, see Michael Aiken and Jerald Hage, "Organizational Alienation: A Comparative Analysis," *American Sociological Review,* 31 (August 1966), 497–507.

15. For a careful definition of these and related terms, see Oscar Oeser and Frank Harary, "Role Structures: A Description in Terms of Graph Theory," in Bruce Biddle and Edwin Thomas (eds.), *Role Theory: Concepts and Research* (New York: Wiley, 1966), pp. 92–102.

16. Among many examples that could be cited, the following are the more interesting because they provide examples of sociological propositions about organizations: Caplow, *Principles of Organization, op. cit.;* Charles Perrow, "A Framework for the Comparative Analysis of Organizations," *American Sociological Review,* 32 (April 1967) 194–208; Jerald Hage, "An Axiomatic Theory of Organization," *Administrative Science Quarterly,* 10 (December 1965), 289–321.

17. Perhaps the best example is James March and Herbert A. Simon, *Organizations* (New York: Wiley, 1958).

18. Harold Guetzkow, "Communications in Organizations," in James March (ed.), *Handbook of Organizations* (Chicago: Rand McNally, 1965), pp. 534–574. The idea of leadership is also important. See, for example, Robert H. Guest, *Organizational Change: The Effects of Successful Leadership* (Homewood, Ill.: Dorsey Press, 1962) and Philip Selznick, *Leadership in Administration* (Evanston, Ill.: Row, Peterson, and Company, 1957).

19. See Dorwin Cartwright, "Influence, Leadership, Control," in March (ed.), *op. cit.,* pp. 1–48; Robert Golembiewski, "Small Groups and Large Organizations," *ibid.,* pp. 87–142; and Abraham Zaleznik, "Interpersonal Relations in Organizations," *ibid.,* pp. 574–614. These titles themselves provide excellent illustrations for some of the topics that interest the social psychologist.

20. See Joseph Massie, "Management Theory," *ibid.,* pp. 387–423; Thomas Marschak, "Economic Theories of Organization," *ibid.,* pp. 423–451; and Julian Feldman and Herschel Kanter, "Organizational Decision-Making," *ibid.,* pp. 614–650. In addition, current issues of *Harvard Business Review, Fortune,* and *Human Organization* provide excellent case studies. Naturally, each of the journals in the disciplines also has articles relevant to the study of organizations. The main journal devoted to the interdisciplinary study of organizations is

Administrative Science Quarterly; each issue provides examples of how these different perspectives can meaningfully contribute to an understanding of the complexity of organizations.

21. See the introduction to the section on change in Etzioni, *op. cit.*, pp. 341–343. An empirical example of this point is John Tsouderos, "Organizational Change in Terms of a Series of Selected Variables," *American Sociological Review,* 20 (April 1955), 206–210.

22. For a discussion of some other organizational characteristics, see Derek S. Pugh, *et al.*, "A Conceptual Scheme for Organizational Analysis," *Administrative Science Quarterly,* 8 (December 1963), 289–316. Actually, most of the organizational variables that they discuss are included in our study, although we have not necessarily used their labels.

23. James Price, "Use of New Knowledge in Organizations," *Human Organization,* 23 (Fall 1964), 224–234.

24. Jerald Hage, *Professional Specialization, and the Problems of Professional Power and Control* (unpublished monograph, University of Wisconsin, 1969), Chapter 1.

25. William J. Goode, "Encroachment, Charlatanism, and the Emerging Profession: Psychology, Sociology, and Medicine," *American Sociological Review,* 25 (December 1960), 902–914.

26. Emile Durkheim, *The Division of Labor in Society,* George Simpson (tr.), (Glencoe, Ill.: Free Press, 1949), Part II.

27. Talcott Parsons, *Societies: Evolutionary and Comparative Perspectives* (Englewood Cliffs, N. J.: Prentice-Hall, 1966).

28. Caplow, *The Sociology of Work, op. cit.*, and March and Simon, *op. cit.*

29. Michel Crozier, *The Bureaucratic Phenomenon* (Chicago: University of Chicago Press, 1964). A more social psychological approach is represented by Chris Argyris, "The Process of Influence and Manipulation Within the Organizational Setting," *Industrial Medicine and Surgery,* 33 (December 1964), 920–928.

30. Max Weber, *The Theory of Social and Economic Organization,* A. M. Henderson and T. Parsons (trs.), (Glencoe, Ill.: Free Press, 1947), especially the section on types of imperative authority.

31. *Ibid.*, p. 337.

32. Robert Presthus, *The Organizational Society: An Analysis and a Theory* (New York: Knopf, 1962).

33. S. N. Eisenstadt, "Bureaucracy, Bureaucratization, and De-bureaucratization," *Administrative Science Quarterly*, 4 (December 1959), 302–321; and William Delaney, "The Development and Decline of Patrimonial and Bureaucratic Administration," in *op. cit.*, 7 (March 1963), 458–501.

34. Chester Barnard, "Functions and Pathology of Status Systems in Formal Organizations," in William Foote Whyte (ed.), *Industry and Society* (New York: McGraw-Hill, 1946), pp. 46–83.

35. Caplow, *Principles of Work, op. cit.*, pp. 60–61.

36. William Starbuck, "Organizational Growth and Development," in March (ed.), *op. cit.*, pp. 451–534.

37. Arthur Stinchcombe, "Bureaucratic and Craft Administration of Production: A Comparative Study," *Administrative Science Quarterly*, 4 (September 1959), 168–187.

38. This was one of Weber's main concerns and the main reason he felt that rational-legal authority would become the dominant form in industrialized societies. See Weber, *op. cit.*, pp. 337–339.

2 Program Change

1. See Donald Ross (ed.), *Administration for Adaptability* (New York: Metropolitan School Study Council, 1958) for the review of the series of studies done at Teachers College, Columbia University. See also, Tom Burns and G. M. Stalker, *The Management of Innovation* (London: Tavistock Publications, 1961) for the studies done in Scotland.

2. Each of the major journals in sociology of the past fifteen years was reviewed in attempting to locate studies relevant to these hypotheses. In addition, *Human Organization, Administrative Science Quarterly, Fortune,* and *Human Relations* were also systematically searched. In many instances the primary objective of a research study was not the topic that we abstracted. Two of the few works that deal explicitly with the question of organizational characteristics that are related to innovation are James Q. Wilson, "Innovation in Organization: Notes

Toward a Theory," in James D. Thompson (ed.), *Approaches to Organizational Design* (Pittsburgh: The University of Pittsburgh Press, 1966), pp. 195–216; and Harold Guetzkow, "The Creative Person in Organizations," in Gary A. Steiner (ed.), *Creative Organizations* (Chicago: University of Chicago Press, 1965), pp. 35–45. Neither of these is an empirical study, however.

3. The study was a three-year panel study of innovation in sixteen social welfare and health organizations. The major findings of this study are reported in Michael Aiken and Jerald Hage, "The Relationship Between Organizational Factors and the Acceptance of New Programs" (unpublished report, University of Wisconsin, 1968).

4. Compare Jerald Hage, "An Axiomatic Theory of Organizations," *Administrative Science Quarterly*, 10 (December 1965), 289–321.

5. See Hans Zetterberg, *On Theory and Verification in Sociology*, rev. ed., (Totowa, N. J.: The Bedminster Press, 1963), p. 11. A small change in x produces a small change in y, which in turn affects a small change in x. Thus, a small change in complexity can lead to some increase in program change, which may then lead to a slight increase in the degree of complexity.

6. Harold L. Wilensky, "The Professionalization of Everyone?" *American Journal of Sociology*, 70 (September 1964), 137–158. See also Harold M. Vollmer and Donald M. Mills, *Professionalization* (Englewood Cliffs, N. J.: Prentice-Hall, 1966).

7. Hage, *Professional Specialization, op. cit.*, Chapter 1.

8. Ross (ed.) *op. cit.*

9. Hilton Buley, "Personal Characteristics and Staff Patterns Associated with the Quality of Education" (unpublished Ed.D. dissertation, Teachers College, Columbia University, 1947).

10. Jerald Hage, "Organizational Response to Innovation" (unpublished Ph.D. dissertation, Columbia University, 1963). See also, John Butler and Jerald Hage, "Physician Attitudes Toward a Hospital Program in Medical Education," *The Journal of Medical Education*, 41 (October 1966), 913–946.

11. Jerald Hage and Michael Aiken, "Program Change and Organizational Properties: A Comparative Analysis," *American Journal of Sociology*, 72 (March 1967), 503–519.

12. Burns and Stalker, *op. cit.*

13. Donald C. Pelz, "Some Social Factors Related to Performance in a Research Organization," *Administrative Science Quarterly,* 1 (December 1956), 310–325.

14. George Strauss, "The Set-up Man: A Case Study of Organizational Change," *Human Organization,* 13 (Summer 1954), 17–25.

15. Hage, "Organizational Response to Innovation," *op. cit.*

16. Robert Michels, *Political Parties,* Eden and Cedar Paul (trs.) (Glencoe, Ill.: Free Press, 1958).

17. François Cillié, *Centralization or Decentralization?: A Study in Educational Adaptation* (New York: Teachers College, Columbia University, 1940), especially p. 195.

18. Joseph Ben-David, "Scientific Productivity and Academic Organization in Nineteenth-Century Medicine," in Bernard Barber and Walter Hirsch (eds.), *The Sociology of Science* (New York: Free Press, 1962), pp. 305–328.

19. Alex Nove, *The Soviet Economy* (New York: Praeger, 1966).

20. Seymour M. Lipset, *Agrarian Socialism: The Cooperative Commonwealth Federation in Saskatchewan* (Berkeley: University of California, 1950), Chapter 12.

21. Hage and Aiken, *op. cit.*

22. Robert K. Merton, "Bureaucratic Structure and Personality," in Amitai Etzioni (ed.), *Complex Organizations: A Sociological Reader* (New York: Holt, Rinehart, and Winston, 1960), pp. 48–61.

23. Robert Kahn, *et al.*, *Organizational Stress: Studies in Role Conflict and Ambiguity* (New York: Wiley, 1964), pp. 72–95, 125–136.

24. Hage and Aiken, *op. cit.*

25. Vance Packard, *The Pyramid Climbers* (New York: McGraw-Hill, 1962).

26. Chester Barnard, "Functions and Pathology of Status Systems in Formal Organizations," in William Foote Whyte (ed.), *Industry and Society* (New York: McGraw-Hill, 1946), pp. 46–83.

27. George C. Homans, *The Human Group* (New York: Harcourt, Brace, 1950), pp. 230–280.

28. Ben-David, *op. cit.*

29. Peter Blau and W. Richard Scott, *Formal Organizations: A*

Comparative Approach (San Francisco: Chandler, 1962), Chapter 5.

30. *Ibid.*

31. Norman H. Berkowitz and Warren G. Bennis, "Interaction Patterns in Formal Service-Oriented Organizations," *Administrative Science Quarterly,* 6 (June 1961), 25–50.

32. Clovis Shepard and Paula Brown, "Status, Prestige, and Esteem in a Research Organization," *Administrative Science Quarterly,* 1 (December 1956), 340–360.

33. Harriet Ronken and Paul Lawrence, *Administering Changes: A Case Study of Human Relations in a Factory* (Cambridge, Mass.: Harvard Graduate Business School, 1952).

34. Basil Georgopoulos and Arnold Tannenbaum, "A Study of Organizational Effectiveness," *American Sociological Review,* 22 (October 1957), 534–540.

35. Cillié, *op. cit.,* classifies a number of school programs in terms of the particular kind of organizational performance affected. Centralized schools were most likely to adopt new programs if they affected efficiency; whereas, decentralized schools were most likely to adopt new programs in other areas.

36. Buley, *op. cit.*

37. Cillié, *op. cit.*

38. Mayer Zald, "Organizational Control Structures in Five Correctional Institutions," *American Journal of Sociology,* 68 (November 1962), 335–345.

39. Ronken and Lawrence, *op. cit.*

40. There are, of course, many factors that can affect job morale and satisfaction. See James G. March and Herbert A. Simon, *Organizations* (New York: Wiley, 1958) for a discussion of some factors that affect the motivation to participate in organizations.

41. Lester Coch and John French, Jr., "Overcoming Resistance to Change," *Human Relations,* 1 (August 1948), 512–532.

42. Alvin Gouldner, *Patterns of Industrial Bureaucracy* (Glencoe, Ill.: Free Press, 1954).

43. Peter Blau, *The Dynamics of Bureaucracy: A Study of Interpersonal Relations in Two Government Agencies* (Chicago: University of Chicago Press, 1955).

44. Hage and Aiken, *op. cit.*

45. Floyd C. Mann and L. Richard Hoffman, *Automation and the*

Worker: A Study of Social Change in Power Plants (New York: Henry Holt and Co., 1960); Floyd C. Mann and F. W. Neff, *Managing Major Change in Organizations* (Ann Arbor, Mich.: Foundation for Research on Human Behavior, 1961); and Floyd C. Mann and Lawrence K. Williams, "Observations on the Dynamics of a Change to Electronic Data-Processing Equipment," *Administrative Science Quarterly,* 5 (September 1960), 217–257.

46. Michel Crozier, *The Bureaucratic Phenomenon* (Chicago: The University of Chicago Press, 1964).

3 Styles of Organizational Change

1. Some sociologists seem to think of a social system as only a set of categories for describing social phenomena, for example, Talcott Parsons, *The Social System* (Glencoe, Ill.: Free Press, 1951), but a social system is quite different from the idea of a system as used in the physical sciences, in which a system implies a set of interrelated variables.

2. Burns and Stalker, *op. cit.,* pp. 60–80.

3. Victor Thompson, *Modern Organizations* (New York: Knopf, 1961), Chapter 3.

4. Victor Thompson, "Bureaucracy and Innovation," *Administrative Science Quarterly,* 10 (June 1965), 1–21.

5. Melville Dalton, "Conflicts between Staff and Line Managerial Officers," *American Sociological Review,* 15 (June 1950), 342–351.

6. For additional arguments relating these variables to one another, see Jerald Hage, "An Axiomatic Theory of Organizations," *Administrative Science Quarterly,* 10 (December 1965), 289–321.

7. Max Weber, *The Theory of Social and Economic Organization,* A. M. Henderson and T. Parsons (trs.), (Glencoe, Ill.: Free Press, 1947).

8. Chester Barnard, "Functions and Pathology of Status Systems in Formal Organizations," in William Foote Whyte (ed.), *Industry and Society* (New York: McGraw-Hill, 1946), pp. 46–83.

9. Burns and Stalker, *op. cit.,* especially pp. 119–125.

10. Burns and Stalker, *op. cit.,* Chapter 7.

11. Arthur Stinchcombe, "Bureaucratic and Craft Administration of Production: A Comparative Study," *Administrative Science Quarterly*, 4 (September 1959), 168–187.
12. David Sills, *The Volunteers* (Glencoe, Ill.: Free Press, 1958).
13. *The New York Times*, Section III, August 8, 1965, p. 1.
14. Alfred D. Chandler, Jr., *Strategy and Structure: Chapters in the History of the Industrial Enterprise* (Cambridge, Mass.: The M. I. T. Press, 1962).
15. *Ibid.*
16. *The New York Times*, Section III, August 12, 1962, p. 1.
17. *The New York Times*, May 21, 1962, p. 60.
18. *The New York Times*, Section III, November 29, 1964, p. 5.
19. *The New York Times*, Section III, May 12, 1963, p. 1.
20. *The New York Times*, Section III, October 20, 1963, p. 27.
21. Henry James, *Charles W. Eliot*, Vol. I (New York: Houghton, Mifflin, 1930).
22. Chandler, *op. cit.*
23. Richard McCleery, *Policy Change in Prison Management* (East Lansing: Government Research Bureau, Michigan State University, 1957).
24. Hage, *Professional Specialization, op. cit.*, Part II.
25. Andrew Kover, "Reorganization of an Advertising Agency," *Human Organization*, 22 (Winter 1963–1964), 252–259.

4 Stages and Strategies

1. T. A. Wise, "IBM's $5,000,000,000 Gamble," *Fortune* (September 1966), pp. 118–123.
2. Paul M. Harrison, *The Free Church Tradition: A Study of the Baptist Convention* (Princeton, N.J.: Princeton University Press, 1959), Chapter 2.
3. Burns and Stalker, *op. cit.*, Chapter 7.
4. Seymour M. Lipset, *Agrarian Socialist: The Cooperative Commonwealth Federation in Saskatchewan* (Berkeley, University of California Press, 1950), Chapter 12.
5. Lester Coch and John French, Jr., "Overcoming Resistance to Change," *Human Relations*, 1 (August 1948), 512–532.
6. Milton Greenblatt, Richard York, and Esther Brown, *From Custodial to Therapeutic Patient Care in Mental Hospitals* (New York: Russell Sage Foundation, 1955).

7. McCleery, *op. cit.*

8. Henry James, *op. cit.*

9. John William Burgess, *Reminiscences of an American Scholar* (New York: Columbia University Press, 1934).

10. An exception to this is Barton and Anderson's careful analysis of Richard McCleery's study of the prison. Allen H. Barton and Bo Anderson, "Change in An Organizational System: Formalization of a Qualitative Study," in Amitai Etzioni (ed.), *Complex Organizations: A Sociological Reader* (New York: Holt, Rinehart and Winston, 1961), pp. 400–418.

11. Hage, "Organizational Response," *op. cit.*

12. Thompson, *op. cit.*

13. Butler and Hage, *op. cit.* pp. 913–946.

14. Floyd C. Mann and F. W. Neff, *Managing Major Change in Organizations* (Ann Arbor, Mich.: Foundation for Research on Human Behavior, 1961); Everett Rogers, *Diffusion of Innovations* (New York: Free Press, 1962); and Neil Smelser, *Social Change in the Industrial Revolution: An Application of Theory to the Lancashire Cotton Industry* (Chicago: University of Chicago Press, 1959).

15. Rogers, *op. cit.*, p. 83.

5 Limitations, Predictions, and Problems

1. The best known exponent of this point of view is George Homans, "Bringing Men Back In," *American Sociological Review*, 29 (December 1964), 809–819. In an attack on the weakness of sociological "theories," Homans wrote: Nor is there any assumption that psychological propositions will explain everything social. We shall certainly not be able to explain everything, but our failures will be attributable to lack of factual information or the intellectual machinery for dealing with complexity—though the computers will help us here—and not to the propositions themselves. Nor is there any assumption here of psychological reductionism, though I used to think there was. For reduction implies that there are general sociological propositions that can then be reduced to psychological ones. I now suspect that there are no general sociological propositions, propositions that hold good of all societies or social groups as

such, and that the only general propositions of sociology are in fact psychological.

2. Philip Selznick, *Leadership in Administration* (New York: Harper & Row, 1957), pp. 90–133.

3. Floyd C. Mann and L. Richard Hoffman, *Automation and the Worker: A Study of Social Change in Power Plants* (New York: Henry Holt and Co., 1960).

4. Jerald Hage and Michael Aiken, "Program Change and Organizational Properties: A Comparative Analysis," *American Journal of Sociology,* 72 (March 1967), 503–519.

5. Sister Maria Augusta Neal, *Values and Interests in Social Change* (Englewood Cliffs, N. J.: Prentice-Hall, 1965).

6. Hage and Aiken, *op. cit.*

7. Compare Robert K. Merton, "Bureaucratic Structure and Personality," in Amitai Etzioni (ed.), *Complex Organizations: A Sociological Reader* (New York: Holt, Rinehart and Winston, 1961), pp. 48–61.

8. Selznick, *op. cit.*, and Robert H. Guest, *Organizational Change: The Effects of Successful Leadership* (Homewood, Ill.: Dorsey and Irwin, 1962).

9. Some of the representative works of this viewpoint are David Street, Robert Vinter, and Charles Perrow, *Organizations for Treatment* (New York: Free Press, 1966); Charles Perrow, "Organizational Prestige: Some Functions and Dysfunctions," *American Journal of Sociology,* 66 (January 1961), 335–341; Charles Perrow, "The Analysis of Goals in Complex Organizations," *American Sociological Review,* 26 (December 1961), 854–866. See also many of the articles on the different kinds of organizations in James G. March (ed.), *Handbook of Organizations* (Chicago: Rand McNally, 1965); and Charles Perrow, "Organizational Goals," *International Encyclopedia of the Social Sciences* (New York: Macmillan and Free Press, 1968), pp. 305–311.

10. As examples of this see Milton Greenblatt, Richard York, and Esther Brown, *From Custodial to Therapeutic Patient Care in Mental Hospitals* (New York: Russell Sage Foundation, 1955); and Richard McCleery, *Policy Change in Prison Management* (East Lansing: Government Research Bureau, Michigan State University, 1957).

11. Ernst Cassirer, *Substance and Function and Einstein's Theory of Relativity*, W. C. Swabey and Marie C. Swabey (trs.) (New York: Dover, 1953), especially Chapter 1.

12. Street, Vinter, and Perrow, *op. cit.*, and Mayer Zald, "Comparative Analysis and Measurement of Organizational Goals: The Case of Correctional Institutions for Delinquents," *Sociological Quarterly*, 4 (1963), 206–230.

13. Greenblatt, York, and Brown, *op. cit.*

14. Robert Blauner, *Alienation and Freedom: The Factory Worker and His Industry* (Chicago: The University of Chicago Press, 1964). See also, Denis Pym, "Technology, Effectiveness, and Predisposition Towards Work-Changes Among Mechanical Engineers." *The Journal of Management Studies*, 3 (October 1966), 304–311.

15. Stanley Udy, Jr., *Organization of Work: A Comparative Analysis of Production Among Non-industrial Peoples* (New Haven, Conn.: Human Relations Area File Press, 1959).

16. Joan Woodward, *Industrial Organization: Theory and Practice* (London: Oxford University Press, 1965).

17. There are some implicit hypotheses in Charles Perrow, "A Framework for the Comparative Analysis of Organizations," *American Sociological Review*, 32 (April 1967), 194–208. See also, Edward Harvey, "Technology and the Structure of Organizations," *American Sociological Review*, 33 (April 1968), 247–259.

18. Harvey, *op. cit.*

19. Ronald Lippitt, Jeanne Watson, and Bruce Westley, *The Dynamics of Planned Change* (New York: Harcourt, Brace, and World, 1958); Rensis Likert, *New Patterns of Management* (New York: McGraw-Hill, 1961); Warren G. Bennis, Kenneth D. Benne, and Robert Chin (eds.), *The Planning of Change: Readings in Applied Behavioral Sciences* (New York: Holt, Rinehart and Winston, 1961); Garth N. Jones, "Strategies and Tactics of Planned Organizational Change: A Case Example in the Modernization Process of Traditional Societies," *Human Organization*, 24 (Fall 1965), 192–201; Warren G. Bennis, "Theory and Method in Applying Behavioral Science to Planned Organizational Change," *The Journal of Applied Behavioral Science*, 11 (October-November 1965), 337–360.

20. Harold J. Leavitt, "Applied Organizational Change in Indus-

try: Structural, Technological, and Humanistic Approaches," in March (ed.) *op cit.*, pp. 1144–1171.

21. Derek S. Pugh, *et al.*, "A Conceptual Scheme for Organizational Analysis," *Administrative Science Quarterly*, 8 (December 1963), 289–316.

22. For a discussion of this, see Allen Barton, *Organizational Measurement* (New York: College Entrance Examination Board, 1961). A number of other kinds of organizational properties are discussed by Barton as well, particularly from the point of view of measurement problems.

23. For reviews of the literature, see Peter Blau and W. Richard Scott, *Formal Organizations: A Comparative Approach* (San Francisco: Chandler, 1962), and Richard Hall, "The Concept of Bureaucracy: An Empirical Assessment," *American Journal of Sociology*, 69 (July 1963), 32–40.

24. In several of the studies reported in Chapters 2 and 3, both size and amount of finances available were controlled in so far as they could be. See Joseph Ben-David, "Scientific Productivity and Academic Organization in Nineteenth Century Medicine," in Bernard Barber and Walter Hirsch (eds.), *The Sociology of Science* (New York: Free Press, 1962), pp. 305–328; François Cillié, *Centralization or Decentralization?: A Study in Educational Adaptation* (New York: Teachers College, Columbia University, 1940); and Hage and Aiken, *op. cit.*

25. Udy, *op. cit.*

26. *Ibid.*

27. *The New York Times*, Section III, August 8, 1965, pp. 1, 11.

28. Bernard Berelson, *Graduate Education in the United States* (New York: McGraw-Hill, 1960).

29. William Ogburn, *Social Change* (New York: B. W. Huebsch, Inc., 1922).

Bibliography

Aiken, Michael, and Jerald Hage. "Organizational Alienation: A Comparative Analysis," *American Sociological Review*, Vol. 31 (August 1966).

————. "Organizational Interdependence and Intra-Organizational Structure," *American Sociological Review*, Vol. 33 (December 1968).

Argyris, Chris. "The Process of Influence and Manipulation Within the Organizational Setting," *Industrial Medicine and Surgery*, Vol. 33 (December 1964).

Barnard, Chester. "Functions and Pathology of Status Systems in Formal Organizations," in William Foote Whyte (ed.), *Industry and Society*. New York: McGraw-Hill, 1946.

Barton, Allen. *Organizational Measurement*. New York: College Entrance Examination Board, 1961.

————, and Bo Anderson. "Change in an Organizational System: Formalization of a Qualitative Study," in Amitai Etzioni (ed.), *Complex Organizations: A Sociological Reader*. New York: Holt, Rinehart and Winston, 1961.

Ben-David, Joseph. "Scientific Productivity and Academic Organization in Nineteenth-Century Medicine," in Bernard Barber and Walter Hirsch (eds.), *The Sociology of Science*. New York: Free Press, 1962.

Bennis, Warren G. "Theory and Method in Applying Behavioral Science to Planned Organizational Change," *The Journal of Applied Behavioral Science*, Vol. 11 (October-November 1965).

————, Kenneth D. Benne, and Robert Chin (eds.). *The Planning of Change: Readings in Applied Behavioral Sciences*. New York: Holt, Rinehart and Winston, 1961.

Berelson, Bernard. *Graduate Education in the United States*. New York: McGraw-Hill, 1960.

Berkowitz, Norman H. and Warren G. Bennis. "Interaction Patterns in Formal Service-Oriented Organizations," *Administrative Science Quarterly*, Vol. 6 (June 1961).

Blau, Peter. *The Dynamics of Bureaucracy: A Study of Interpersonal Relations in Two Government Agencies.* Chicago: University of Chicago Press, 1955.

————, and W. Richard Scott. *Formal Organizations: A Comparative Approach.* San Francisco: Chandler, 1962.

Blauner, Robert. *Alienation and Freedom: The Factory Worker and His Industry.* Chicago: University of Chicago Press, 1964.

Blumer, Herbert. "Collective Behavior," in A. M. Lee (ed.), *New Outline of the Principles of Sociology.* New York: Barnes and Noble, 1946.

Brooks, Harvey. "Innovation: The Force Behind Man's March Into the Future," *The New York Times,* January 8, 1968.

Buley, Hilton. "Personal Characteristics and Staff Patterns Associated with the Quality of Education." Unpublished Ed.D. project, Teachers College, Columbia University, 1947.

Burgess, John William. *Reminiscences of an American Scholar.* New York: Columbia University Press, 1934.

Burns, Tom, and G. M. Stalker. *The Management of Innovation.* London: Tavistock Publications, 1961.

Butler, John, and Jerald Hage, "Physician Attitudes Toward a Hospital Program in Medical Education," *The Journal of Medical Education,* Vol. 41 (October 1966).

Caplow, Theodore. *The Sociology of Work.* Minneapolis: University of Minnesota Press, 1954.

————. *Principles of Organization.* New York: Harcourt, Brace & World, 1964.

Cartwright, Dorwin. "Influence, Leadership, Control," in James March (ed.), *Handbook of Organizations.* Chicago: Rand McNally, 1965.

Casimir, H. B. "Gapology, Both Scientific and Managerial, a Cause for Concern in Europe," *The New York Times,* January 8, 1968.

Cassirer, Ernst. *Substance and Function and Einstein's Theory of Relativity.* W. C. Swabey and Marie A. Swabey (trs.). New York: Dover, 1953.

Chandler, A. D., Jr. *Strategy and Structure: Chapters in the History of the Industrial Enterprise.* Cambridge, Mass.: M.I.T. Press, 1962.

Chin, Robert. "The Utility of System Models on Developmental Models for Practioners," in Warren G. Bennis, Kenneth D.

Benne, and Robert Chin (eds.), *The Planning of Change: Readings in Applied Behavioral Sciences.* New York: Holt, Rinehart and Winston, 1961.

Cillié, François. *Centralization or Decentralization: A Study in Educational Adaptation.* New York: Teachers College, Columbia University Press, 1940.

Coch, Lester, and John French, Jr. "Overcoming Resistance to Change," *Human Relations,* Vol. 1 (August 1948).

Cooley, Charles Horton. *Social Organization: A Study of the Larger Mind.* New York: Scribner, 1909.

Crozier, Michel. *The Bureaucratic Phenomenon.* Chicago: University of Chicago Press, 1964.

Dalton, Melville. "Conflicts Between Staff and Line Managerial Officers," *American Sociological Review,* Vol. 15 (June 1950).

Delaney, William. "The Development and Decline of Patrimonial and Bureaucratic Administration," *Administrative Science Quarterly,* Vol. 7 (March 1963).

Dobzhansky, Theodosius. *Mankind Evolving: The Evolution of the Human Species.* New Haven, Conn.: Yale University Press, 1962.

Durkheim, Emile. *The Division of Labor in Society.* George Simpson (tr.). Glencoe, Ill.: Free Press, 1949.

Eisenstadt, S. N. "Bureaucracy, Bureaucratization, and Debureaucratization," *Administrative Science Quarterly.* Vol. 4 (December 1959).

Etzioni, Amitai (ed.), *Complex Organizations: A Sociological Reader.* New York: Holt, Rinehart and Winston, 1961.

Feldman, Julian and Herschel Kanter. "Organizational Decision Making," in James March (ed.), *Handbook of Organizations.* Chicago: Rand McNally, 1965.

Georgopoulos, Basil and Arnold Tannenbaum. "A Study of Organizational Effectiveness," *American Sociological Review,* Vol. 22 (October, 1957).

Georgopoulos, Basil and Floyd Mann. *The Community General Hospital.* New York: Macmillan, 1962.

Golembiewski, Robert. "Small Groups and Large Organizations," in James March (ed.), *Handbook of Organizations.* Chicago: Rand McNally, 1965.

Goode, William J. "Encroachment, Charlatanism, and the Emerging

Profession: Psychology, Sociology, and Medicine," *American Sociological Review*, Vol. 25 (December 1960).

Gouldner, Alvin. *Patterns of Industrial Bureaucracy*. Glencoe, Ill.: Free Press, 1954.

Greenblatt, Milton, Richard York, and Esther Brown. *From Custodial to Therapeutic Patient Care in Mental Hospitals: Explorations in Social Treatment*. New York: Russell Sage Foundation, 1955.

Greiner, Larry E. "Patterns of Organizational Change," *Harvard Business Review*, Vol. 45(3) (May-June, 1967).

————. "Organization Change and Development: A Study of Changing Values, Behavior and Performance in a Large Industrial Plant." Unpublished Ph.D. dissertation, Graduate School of Business Administration, Harvard University, February 1965.

Guest, Robert H. *Organizational Change: The Effects of Successful Leadership*. Homewood, Ill.: Dorsey Press, 1962.

Guetzkow, Harold. "The Creative Person in Organizations," in Gary A. Steiner (ed.). *The Creative Organization*. Chicago: University of Chicago Press, 1965.

————. "Communications in Organizations," in James March (ed.), *Handbook of Organizations*. Chicago: Rand McNally, 1965.

Hage, Jerald. "Organizational Response to Innovation." Unpublished Ph.D. dissertation, Columbia University, 1963.

————. "An Axiomatic Theory of Organization," *Administrative Science Quarterly*, Vol. 10 (December 1965).

————. *Professional Specialization, and the Problems of Professional Power and Control*. Unpublished monograph, University of Wisconsin, 1969.

————, and Michael Aiken. "Program Change and Organizational Properties: A Comparative Analysis," *American Journal of Sociology*, Vol. 72 (March 1967).

Hall, Richard. "Intraorganizational Structural Variation: Application of the Bureaucratic Model," *Administrative Science Quarterly*, Vol. 7 (December 1962).

————. "The Concept of Bureaucracy: An Empirical Assessment," *American Journal of Sociology*, Vol. 69 (July 1963).

Harvey, Edward. "Technology and the Structure of Organizations," *American Sociological Review*, Vol. 33 (April 1968).

Harrison, Paul M. *Authority and Power* in the *Free Church Tradition*. Princeton, N. J.: Princeton University Press, 1959.

Heirich, Max. "The Use of Time in the Study of Social Change," *American Sociological Review,* Vol. 29 (June 1964).

Homans, George. "Bringing Men Back In," *American Sociological Review,* Vol. 29 (December 1964).

James, Henry. *Charles W. Eliot*. 2 Vols. New York: Houghton Mifflin, 1930.

Jones, Garth N. "Strategies and Tactics of Planned Organizational Change," *Human Organization,* Vol. 24 (Fall 1965).

Kahn, Robert, *et al. Organizational Stress: Studies in Role Conflict and Ambiguity*. New York: Wiley, 1964.

LaPiere, Richard T. *Collective Behavior*. New York: McGraw-Hill, 1938.

Lazarsfeld, Paul, and Wagner Thielens, Jr. *The Academic Mind*. Glencoe, Ill.: Free Press, 1958.

Leavitt, Harold J. "Applied Organizational Change in Industry: Structural, Technological, and Humanistic Approaches," in James G. March (ed.), *Handbook of Organizations*. Chicago: Rand McNally, 1965.

Likert, Rensis. *New Patterns of Management*. New York: McGraw-Hill, 1961.

————. *The Human Organization: Its Management and Value*. New York: McGraw-Hill, 1967.

Lippitt, Ronald, Jean Watson, and Bruce Westley. *The Dynamics of Planned Change*. New York: Harcourt, Brace & World, 1958.

Lipset, Seymour M. *Agrarian Socialism: The Cooperative Commonwealth Federation in Saskatchewan*. Berkeley: University of California Press, 1950.

————. *Political Man*. Garden City, N. Y.: Doubleday, 1960.

Lorsch, Jay W., and Paul Lawrence. "Organizing for Product Innovation," *Harvard Business Review,* Vol. 43 (January-February 1965).

Mann, Floyd C., and L. Richard Hoffman. *Automation and the Worker: A Study of Social Change in Power Plants*. New York: Henry Holt & Co., 1960.

————, and F. W. Neff. *Managing Major Change in Organizations*. Ann Arbor, Mich.: Foundation for Research on Human Behavior, 1961.

————, and Lawrence K. Williams. "Observations on the Dynamics of a Change to Electronic Data-processing Equipment," *Administrative Science Quarterly*, Vol. 5 (September 1960).

March, James G. *Handbook of Organizations*. Chicago: Rand McNally, 1965.

————, and Herbert A. Simon. *Organizations*. New York: Wiley, 1958.

Marschak, Thomas. "Economic Theories of Organization," in James G. March (ed.), *Handbook of Organizations*. Chicago: Rand McNally, 1965.

Massie, Joseph. "Management Theory," in James G. March (ed.), *Handbook of Organizations*. Chicago: Rand McNally, 1965.

McCleery, Richard. *Policy Change in Prison Management*. East Lansing, Mich.: Government Research Bureau, Michigan State University, 1957.

Merton, Robert K. "Bureaucratic Structure and Personality," in Amitai Etzioni (ed.), *Complex Organizations: A Sociological Reader*. New York: Holt, Rinehart and Winston, 1961.

————. *Social Theory and Social Structure*. Rev. ed. Glencoe, Ill.: Free Press, 1957.

Michels, Robert. *Political Parties*. Eden and Cedar Paul (trs.), Glencoe, Ill.: Free Press, 1958.

Morse, Nancy, and Everett R. Reimer. "The Experimental Change of a Major Organizational Variable," *Journal of Abnormal and Social Psychology*, Vol. 52 (1956).

Neal, Sister Maria Augusta. *Values and Interests in Social Change*. Englewood Cliffs, N. J.: Prentice-Hall, 1965.

Nove, Alec. *The Soviet Economy*. New York: Praeger, 1966.

Oeser, Oscar, and Frank Harary. "Role Structures: A Description in Terms of Graph Theory," in Bruce Biddle and Edwin Thomas (eds.), *Role Theory: Concepts and Research*. New York: Wiley, 1966.

Ogburn, William. *Social Change*. New York: B. W. Huebsch, 1922.

Packard, Vance. *The Pyramid Climbers*. New York: McGraw-Hill, 1962.

Parsons, Talcott. *The Social System*. Glencoe, Ill.: Free Press, 1951.

————. "Sociological Approach to the Theory of Organizations," *Administrative Science Quarterly*, Vol. 1 (June 1956).

————. "General Theory in Sociology," in Robert Merton, Leonard

Broom, and Leonard Cottrell, Jr. (eds.), *Sociology Today*. New York: Basic Books, 1959.

————. *Structure and Process in Modern Societies*. Glencoe, Ill.: Free Press, 1960.

————. *Societies: Evolutionary and Comparative Perspectives*. Englewood Cliffs, N. J.: Prentice-Hall, 1966.

————, Robert F. Bales, and Edward A. Shils. *Working Papers in the Theory of Action*. Glencoe, Ill.: Free Press, 1953.

————, Edward A. Shils, and Edward C. Tolman. *Toward a General Theory of Action*. Cambridge, Mass.: Harvard University Press, 1949.

Pearlin, Leonard, and Morris Rosenberg. "Nurse-Patient Social Distance and the Structural Context of a Mental Hospital," *American Sociological Review*, Vol. 27 (February 1962).

Pelz, Donald C. "Some Social Factors Related to Performance in a Research Organization," *Administrative Science Quarterly*, Vol. 1 (December 1956).

Perrow, Charles. "Organizational Prestige: Some Functions and Dysfunctions," *American Journal of Sociology*, Vol. 66 (January 1961).

————. "The Analysis of Goals in Complex Organizations," *American Sociological Review*, Vol. 26 (December 1961).

————. "A Framework for the Comparative Analysis of Organizations," *American Sociological Review*, Vol. 32 (April 1967).

————. "Organizational Goals," in *International Encyclopedia of the Social Sciences*. Vol. II. New York: Macmillan Free Press, 1968.

Presthus, Robert. *The Organizational Society: An Analysis and a Theory*. New York: Knopf, 1962.

Price, James. "Use of New Knowledge in Organizations," *Human Organizations*, Vol. 23 (Fall 1964).

Pugh, D. S., *et al.* "A Conceptual Scheme for Organizational Analysis," *Administrative Science Quarterly*, Vol. 8 (December 1963).

Pym, Denis. "Technology, Effectiveness, and Predisposition Towards Work-Changes Among Mechanical Engineers," *The Journal of Management Studies*, Vol. 3 (October 1966).

Redfield, Robert. *The Folk Culture of Yucatan*. Chicago: University of Chicago Press, 1941.

Rogers, Everett. *Diffusion of Innovations*. New York: Free Press, 1962.

Ronken, Harriet, and Paul Lawrence. *Administering Changes: A Case Study of Human Relations in a Factory*. Cambridge, Mass.: Harvard Graduate Business School, 1952.

Ross, Donald (ed.). *Administration for Adaptability*. New York: Metropolitan School Study Council, 1958.

Seeman, Melvin, and John Evans. "Stratification and Hospital Care: The Performance of the Medical Intern," *American Sociological Review*, Vol. 26 (February 1961).

Selznick, Philip. *Leadership in Administration*. New York: Harper & Row, 1957.

Shepard, Clovis, and Paula Brown. "Status, Prestige, and Esteem in a Research Organization," *Administrative Science Quarterly*, Vol. 1 (December 1956).

Sills, David. *The Volunteers*. Glencoe, Ill.: Free Press, 1958.

Sloan, Alfred P., Jr. "My Years with General Motors—Part 1," *Fortune* (September 1963).

Smelser, Neil J. *Social Change in the Industrial Revolution: An Application of Theory to the Lancashire Cotton Industry*. Chicago: University of Chicago Press, 1959.

————. *Theory of Collective Behavior*. New York: Free Press, 1963.

Smith, Richard. "How a Great Corporation Got out of Control," two parts, *Fortune* (January 1962) and (February 1962).

Starbuck, William. "Organizational Growth and Development," in James G. March (ed.), *Handbook of Organizations*. Chicago: Rand McNally, 1965.

Steiner, Gary A. (ed.). *Creative Organizations*. Chicago: University of Chicago Press, 1965.

Stinchcombe, Arthur. "Bureaucratic and Craft Administration of Production: A Comparative Study," *Administrative Science Quarterly*, Vol. 4 (September 1959).

Strauss, George. "The Set-up Man: A Case Study of Organizational Change," *Human Organization*, Vol. 13 (Summer 1954).

Street, David, Robert Vinter, and Charles Perrow. *Organization for Treatment*. New York: Free Press, 1966.

Teilhard de Chardin, Pierre. *The Phenomenon of Man*. Bernard Wall (tr.). New York: Harper & Row, 1959.

Thompson, Victor. *Modern Organization.* New York: Knopf, 1961.
————. "Bureaucracy and Innovation," *Administrative Science Quarterly,* Vol. 10 (June 1965).

Touraine, Alain, *et al. Workers' Attitudes to Technical Change: An Integrated Survey of Research.* Paris: Organization for Economic Co-operation and Development, 1965.

Tsouderos, John. "Organizational Change in Terms of a Series of Selected Variables," *American Sociological Review,* Vol. 20 (April 1955).

Turner, Ralph, and Lewis M. Killian. *Collective Behavior.* Englewood Cliffs, N.J.: Prentice-Hall, 1957.

Udy, Stanley, Jr. *Organization of Work: A Comparative Analysis of Production Among Nonindustrial Peoples.* New Haven: Human Relations Area File Press, 1959.

Walker, Charles R. *Toward the Automatic Factory: A Case Study of Men and Machines.* New Haven, Conn.: Yale University Press, 1957.

Weber, Max. *The Theory of Social and Economic Organization.* A. Henderson and T. Parsons (trs.). Glencoe, Ill.: Free Press, 1947.

Whyte, William H. *The Organizational Man.* New York: Simon and Schuster, 1956.

Wilensky, Harold, and Charles Lebeaux. *Industrial Society and Social Welfare.* New York: Russell Sage Foundation, 1958.

Wilson, James Q. "Innovation in Organization: Notes Toward a Theory," in James D. Thompson (ed.), *Approaches to Organizational Design.* Pittsburgh, Pa.: University of Pittsburgh Press, 1966.

Woodward, Joan. *Industrial Organization: Theory and Practice.* London: Oxford University Press, 1965.

Zald, Mayer. "Comparative Analysis and Measurement of Organizational Goals: The Case of Correctional Institutions for Delinquents," *Sociological Quarterly,* Vol. 4 (Winter 1963).
————. "Organizational Control Structures in Five Correctional Institutions," *American Journal of Sociology,* Vol. 68 (November 1962).
————, and Patricia Denton. "The Transformation of the YMCA: From Evangelism to General Service," *Administrative Science Quarterly,* Vol. 8 (September 1963).

Zaleznik, Abraham. "Interpersonal Relations in Organizations," in

James G. March (ed.), *Handbook of Organizations*. Chicago: Rand McNally, 1965.

Zetterberg, Hans. *On Theory and Verification in Sociology*. Rev. ed. Totowa, N. J.: Bedminster Press, 1963.

Index